BF
TROUBLED WATERS

A Memoir

To Angelia alla
Lee

PAMELA E. BRIDGEWATER

Pam E Bright
7/25

BK
ROYSTON
Publishing

BK Royston Publishing
Jeffersonville, IN

© Copyright – 2025

Editor: Mark Olson

Cover Design: Pamela E. Bridgewater and Marvin H. Jackson

Cover Artist: Sergio Drumond

Cover Photography: Kevin Pryor

ISBN: 978-1-967282-03-6

LCCN: 2025904494

Printed in the United States of America

DEDICATION

To the late U.S. Ambassador John Burroughs, a trailblazer who started me on this journey and convinced me that I could be a diplomat who made a positive difference.

To the late U.S. Ambassador William Lacy Swing, who supported my assignment to apartheid South Africa as the only African American officer in the embassy's political section and gave me outstanding opportunities to grow and showcase my talents fully.

To the late U.S. Ambassador Johnny Young who believed I could be consul general in Durban, South Africa and advocated for my assignment there.

To the late U.S. Ambassador Princeton N. Lyman who supported my assignment as consul general in Durban, South Africa at a critical point in that country's historic transition from apartheid.

To the late Cheryl Hodge and Janice Clements who helped me and scores of other diplomats understand the nuances of the assignment and evaluation process at the Department of State, helping U.S. to make wise and career-enhancing assignment choices.

TABLE OF CONTENTS

FOREWORD

Ambassador Pamela E. Bridgewater, a trailblazing figure in American diplomacy, has shared her life story and insights in "Bridging Troubled Waters." My dear friend and colleague's memoir reflects her extraordinary career, including her close and productive relationship with Nelson Mandela.

The Ambassador details her journey from segregated Fredericksburg, Virginia to becoming an ingenious Foreign Service Officer. Her life is one of perseverance and doggedness, defeating systematic racism and professional hurdles to rise to the top ranks of the Foreign Service, the world's most elite diplomatic corps.

Ambassador Bridgewater offers a straightforward and cogent window into her role in navigating U.S. - South Africa relations during one of the most critical periods in global history. Her work as the first African American woman Consul General in Durban, combatting apartheid, contributed to fostering engagements and supporting South Africa's transition to democracy.

The memoir also highlights Ambassador Bridgewater's accomplishments as Ambassador to Benin, Ghana and Jamaica, as well as her work as a deputy assistant secretary in the African Affairs Bureau of the U.S. Department of State. Throughout her groundbreaking book, Bridgewater stresses the importance of faith, diplomacy, education and cultural understanding in addressing personal and global hurdles.

—U.S. Ambassador Harry K. Thomas, Jr.

PREFACE

As far back as I can remember, being diplomatic seemed "natural" to me, even though I wasn't sure as a teenager exactly what that meant. One of our beloved youth leaders, Mrs. Gladys P. Todd, would often say, "Pamey, you're a real diplomat." Mrs. Todd was an educator and youth advisor who ran the summer playground at our City Park during summer vacations and she was a member of our family church, Shiloh Baptist Church (Old Site).

She had frequent opportunities to observe me growing up and often used the "diplomat" description of me when she heard arguments or squabbles among the children on some issue. She observed that I always seemed to produce an answer or solution that met all our needs -- a compromise, suggestion or solution that made everyone feel like a winner.

Mrs. Todd passed away in 2015 at the age of one hundred-two knowing that her prediction of my diplomatic capabilities and potential had come to fruition. Her daughter, Gaye Todd Adegbalola, later told me that her mom always enjoyed hearing the latest news of my diplomatic journey.

I suppose it was a good thing for me to hear of my "diplomatic abilities" as a young child, although I was not quite sure what that was at that time. I do not recall that I ever in fact looked up the word diplomat, but owing to my interest in international and national affairs, I watched news reports and was always glued to the work of U.S. ambassadors and other officials, particularly as it related to their international engagements. Still, I never thought that I would become an actual diplomat, and certainly not a three-time United States Ambassador representing U.S. presidents, William J. "Bill" Clinton, George W. Bush, and Barack H. Obama. My early aspiration was to become a lawyer after studying political science, history and geography. However, during my teen years, I remember reading the exciting *Scholastic Magazine* news reports about international events that always brought such delight to me.

Bridging Troubled Waters recalls the unimaginable experiences of a young black girl from segregated Fredericksburg, Virginia, who became an accomplished and decorated U.S. Diplomat. There were frequent unlikely encounters with world leaders, history makers and citizens from all sectors of society, advocating for youth educational opportunities, especially for women and girls. I witnessed incredible transforming developments on the world scene, and crossed many troubled waters I could never have fathomed bridging.

I was introduced to the honorable Nelson Mandela, in a warm setting, shortly after my unplanned diplomatic posting in Pretoria, South Africa. This was the beginning of a very special friendship with the international freedom fighting icon. There I was, participating and strategizing with colleagues and South Africans in the midst of dismantling apartheid.

Witnessing the end of this system of discrimination on grounds of race and helping forge new structures of non-racial government and economic empowerment became the most exciting and unforgettable period of my diplomatic career. I encountered Mr. Mandela ten years after I joined the Foreign Service at the urging of U.S. Ambassador John Burroughs. From that initial meeting, Mr. Mandela and I developed a special rapport that continued throughout my six-year assignment in South Africa. It helped set the stage for an unimaginable career nonpareil.

Bridging Troubled Waters chronicles the story of my ordinary small-town beginning in Fredericksburg, Virginia. I will explore my relationship with Mr. Mandela in detail. It is a journey that has taken me to six continents, while negotiating with rebel leaders, helping to forge peace, strengthening democratic governance and spreading hope, goodwill, compassion and cultural diplomacy along the way.

Thank you for journeying with me as we share this memoir, with assistance from my distinguished diplomatic colleagues who helped me recall the alluring details of this remarkable story. You will see why it was an honor for me to strengthen ties between the peoples of the world, and to positively impact the foreign policy objectives of the United States of America.

CHAPTER 1

THE BEGINNING

My journey began upon my birth at 515 Amelia Street in the historic city of Fredericksburg, Virginia. Fredericksburg was known for many things. It was the boyhood home of President George Washington; President James Monroe practiced law here; and the Statute for Religious Freedom was signed in a neighborhood near where I was born. One of the bloodiest battles of the Civil War was fought in Fredericksburg when Union soldiers suffered a crushing defeat. It was also a city where enslaved persons from the continent of Africa were purchased and sold at auction downtown on an infamous stone-block site. The auction block was removed and is now located in the Fredericksburg

Area Museum with explanations of its ugly history, but I remember walking past that stone block nearly every day. It was also a city where brave individuals escaped slavery by way of the "Liberty Line" an underground railway route that led them to freedom in the North, via the Rappahannock River, which runs through Fredericksburg. My neighborhood was also close to the Kenmore Plantation, owned by Betty Washington, George's sister and her husband, an owner of enslaved persons.

There was nothing exceptional about the conditions and circumstances of my birth. Those aboard my lifeboat were my mother, Mary Elizabeth Hester Bridgewater, and my grandparents, Rev. Dr. B. H. Hester and Mrs. Blanche Elizabeth Alexander Hester. My aunt Mildred ("Mamie") also lived in our home. The story is told that my mother couldn't wait to get to the hospital for my delivery. I was quite impatient to get going with my life (and still am impatient), according to her accounts, and those of Dr. R.C. Ellison, MD,

one of our ci..,
at the family home. ...ring black doctors, who delivered me
...her, Joseph Nathaniel Bridge-
water, an acclaimed jazz trum,. ...,yer, was not present for
my birth. He was "on the road" perfor.. ..., as he often was,
with famed musical groups including legends like Ray
Charles.

With my mom, Mary Elizabeth Hester Bridgewater

one of our city's pioneering black doctors, who delivered me at the family home. My father, Joseph Nathaniel Bridgewater, an acclaimed jazz trumpet player, was not present for my birth. He was "on the road" performing, as he often was, with famed musical groups including legends like Ray Charles.

With my mom, Mary Elizabeth Hester Bridgewater

With my father, Joseph Nathaniel Bridgewater

Like many black children, I was nurtured by my mother, grandparents and maternal aunt in a warm, supportive, and loving environment as an only child and only grandchild. 515 Amelia Street, which I will refer to henceforth as "515," was the parsonage of the historic Shiloh Baptist Church (Old Site) in Fredericksburg where my grandfather served as pastor for forty years. The house was built in 1912 by Rev. J. C. Diamond, a master architect and builder who was pastor of the Shiloh Baptist Church (Old Site), prior to the pastorate of my grandfather.

Our home at 515 Amelia Street, Fredericksburg, Virginia

In researching the parsonage, I learned that two lots adjacent to it on the right and on the left, had been owned by a former enslaved man. His name was George Brook (or Brooks as sometimes documented), and he had been freed from slavery in 1835. The original line of ownership for 515 was recorded in the Husting Court of Fredericksburg. Historic Fredericksburg Foundation, Inc., researched the property and designated it as a *Century Home*. It has been renovated beautifully by a young Ghanaian civil engineer, Victor Quaye. The vintage house built by Rev. Diamond had to meet certain architectural and design standards to be considered as a century home.

My grandfather arrived in Fredericksburg in 1922 to pastor the original Shiloh Baptist Church (Old Site). He met his wife Blanche (my grandmother) while he was a teacher and principal at the Mayfield High School in Fredericksburg, the only place black students could matriculate at the time. She was a student, twelve years his junior. They would be together for the next fifty-two years.

Students who graduated from Mayfield High only needed two additional years to receive a bachelor's degree, a forerunner of today's advanced placement courses, I'd say.

My grandfather was born the son of John Henry Hester, my great grandfather, an enslaved man who resided in Oxford, North Carolina. Granddaddy earned two baccalaureate degrees (Biddle University, now Johnson C. Smith University, and Virginia Union University); and an honorary Doctor of Divinity (Virginia Union University), all historically black colleges and universities (HBCUs). He was also a founding member of the Omega Psi Phi Fraternity, Inc., Iota Chapter at Virginia Union. It is one of the oldest African American Greek letter fraternities. My granddaddy's story is a testament to the importance of HBCUs at that time, and they are still extremely important now.

My grandfather was not only a pastor and teacher, but a social activist, author and fighter for the rights of black citizens. His carefully crafted editorials to local and state newspapers opposing injustices for black citizens yielded positive results. He established a night school to teach literacy, so that blacks in Fredericksburg could learn to read and write and be eligible to *vote*. When I retired from the Foreign Service, I found many materials my mother had saved. While perusing these original documents, I learned of his prowess with the pen. I was fascinated and prompted to write about his accomplishments. The book, published in 2016, is entitled *Neutral on Nothing: The Social Activism of the Rev. B. H. Hester.* In retrospect, I was inspired as I watched him proficiently and diplomatically navigating his work as a Baptist pastor, addressing congregational concerns and societal issues. Was this a foreshadowing of the diplomatic profession I would later encumber?

My grandmother, Blanche, was a high school graduate, but her adept knowledge of advanced mathematics, algebra and physics was extensive; I would turn to her for help with my homework for complicated physics and algebra during my high school days. She always easily explained how to solve the problems so that I could understand. She was, also, a licensed practical nurse, working at Fredericksburg's segregated Mary Washington Hospital in the pediatric division for over thirty years before her retirement. She actively promoted women's reproductive rights and equal rights very early on and joined with other female activists such as Mrs. Lettie Ellison (wife of Dr. R. C. Ellison). I remember her stories of administering vaccines against typhoid during the many destructive floods of the Rappahannock River on whose banks the Shiloh Baptist Church (Old Site) stood. She played piano for the Sunday school, sang in the choir, and sometimes attempted to play our beautiful Moller organ when the regular organist was ill. Multitasking for women did not just begin. I witnessed it every day growing up. She was a woman for all seasons.

My mom, Mary Elizabeth, the firstborn, attended the private Mary Potter Boarding School in Oxford, North Carolina, her birthplace, before completing high school at the Walker-Grant High School, which was the original Mayfield High School. She attended Virginia Union University in

Richmond, Virginia. When she and my father divorced and she relocated to Fredericksburg, mom worked as a domestic and then trained at the local Mary Washington Hospital to become a nurse's aide. She worked in the obstetrics department for over twenty years.

She changed careers in the 1960s and became Fredericksburg's first black bank teller at The National Bank of Fredericksburg and retired after twenty-five years. She was the darling and favorite of customers, who would wait to be attended by her despite the availability of shorter lines. She always had a lollipop for children with parents' permission and dog biscuits for canine friends. Mom received numerous awards for her performance excellence in teller services. Upon retiring, she maintained her service ethic, helping to establish a community clinic at a local housing complex, going from house to house to take blood pressure readings for others not living in the housing complex, and serving her fellow men and women in their times of need. Serving and caring were her trademarks.

Aunt Mildred (Mamie) and Uncle Gandhi (somehow, I never referred to them as aunt and uncle), the second and third of Mom's siblings, were schoolteachers and graduates of Johnson C. Smith University and Virginia Union University, respectively. Mamie later studied at New York University and received a master's degree in education. She taught third grade at the John J. Wright Consolidated School in Spotsylvania County, Virginia. Gandhi served in the US Army and upon discharge began teaching in Saluda, Virginia, in the western part of the state, and later at King George High School in King George, Virginia. After his retirement from teaching, Gandhi worked for the State of Virginia Circuit Court. Over the years, both Mamie and Gandhi were instrumental in shaping the lives of hundreds of young black students in these two formerly segregated school systems.

My childhood journeys were full of fun and mischief. Many of my childhood playmates and fellow schoolmates are today my lifelong friends; however, my formative days in Fredericksburg in the late 1940s and onward were characterized and defined by the legal segregation of black and white—in schools, churches, eating and public accommodations—a situation which defined the southern United States. During those years, I knew very little about my grandfather's social activism while bridging the troubled waters he faced.

"Walker-Grant Oh Walker-Grant, Oh that's the Place for Me!"

Those words from my elementary and high school Alma Mater will forever have a place in my memory for many reasons. I walked over two miles from home, passing by Maury Elementary School, which was for whites only, and a few blocks from my home neighborhood, to get to the all-black, segregated Walker-Grant School. Our dear school was named for two distinguished black educators, Joseph Walker and Jason Grant. Nearby, was the Lafayette Elementary School, also for white children only. It was a good half-hour walk to the "colored" Walker-Grant school, built near the Gunnery Spring. The 10:10 a.m. recess was of course a favorite time as we ran and played for fifteen glorious minutes up and down the green, greasy hill, enjoying the playground equipment and panting out of breath. We slowed down only to cup our hands for a cool refreshing drink from the constantly running Gunnery Spring. The words Walker-Grant School for Colored remained on the school façade for years before it was removed.

Those early memories and experiences painted my tableau of what racial discrimination was about. Notwithstanding the unfairness, what good did I find at Walker-Grant on the other side of the tracks? Well, it was the role-model teachers who were successful despite the obstacles they faced and overcame, not because of birthright or heredity but because of perseverance, intestinal fortitude and keen intellect.

I found a learning environment that was nurturing, and teachers who were first-rate and caring. They were stern and no-nonsense. Our resources and materials were never equal to those of James Monroe, Lafayette or Maury, the "white" schools, but we made up for it with teachers like Marguerite Bailey Young, Margaret Brown Whylie, Louise Jeter Lucas, Mamie Boykin Scott, Virginia B. Kay, Lucille Robinson, Lelia Clark, Johnny P. Johnson, Blonnie P. Tipton, William Stephens, Barbara M. Weston, and Janie Mae Pratt (my first-grade teacher). The French language skills I learned from Mrs. Whylie were second to none and enabled me to use them in the diplomatic career that I pursued later in life.

My love of classical and other musical genre was nurtured by Mrs. Tipton, our extraordinary music teacher. My fellow band members recall that all I had to do was get a piece of music one time and I had memorized it quickly, not needing to use music for our marching and concert bank performances. Our highly decorated marching and concert bands were always first-place winners in local and state competitions. We often were rated Superior plus, plus!! And what our teachers taught us, both by precept and example, instilled in all of us the belief that we *could and would* achieve greatly and be able to attend an Ivy League university like Yale or Princeton, or HBCUs like Hampton and Virginia State. We did! What a foundation!

I participated in peaceful civil-rights protests at the height of the civil-rights movement and in the 1960s. What I saw imparted in me as a teenager the right and obligation to peacefully protest social injustice, for example, segregated lunch counters and eating facilities. I sat in and picketed with other young people at the downtown Woolworth, People's Drug (now CVS) and W.T. Grant stores. Our mentors and counselors were church leaders such as Dr. Phillip Y. Wyatt, a black dentist and national civil-rights activist in the NAACP, and the Rev. Lawrence Davies, who served as pastor of Shiloh Baptist Church (Old Site) for fifty years after my grandfather Rev. Hester. Rev. Davies was also elected the first black mayor of Fredericksburg and remained the longest serving mayor of our city, serving for twenty years until his death in 2024. Mrs. Gladys P. Todd, Mrs. Marguerite Bailey Young, Mr. Johnny P. Johnson and Mr. William Wright were among many other leaders who guided our youthful activism to successful outcomes. I remember receiving life-altering and wise mentoring, guidance and nurturing (including many scoldings) from family, teachers and community leaders. From an incredibly early age, I experienced the importance of education, including the exposure to classic books, music and the arts, all experiences that have defined me throughout my life.

Seeing the examples of my family from birth, I was confident that though I would certainly face challenges and obstacles along the way, I was equipped, empowered, capable and ready to take them on headfirst and overcome them. I was not fully aware, however, of how much I was following in the tradition of my family elders treading through the waters they forged and bridges they had crossed.

CHAPTER 2

HAIL STATE! HAIL!

I graduated from Walker-Grant in 1964 as the class salutatorian and Wilfred Lucas was valedictorian. There were a whopping 15 members of the class. Although 515 was only a short walk from a top-rated college—Mary Washington, now the University of Mary Washington—the segregation of educational facilities in Virginia remained the law, and blacks were not allowed to matriculate there. Dr. Samuel DeWitt Proctor, noted educator, pastor, and distant relative, recommended that I apply to Virginia State College (now Virginia State University), an HBCU in Petersburg, Virginia. It was the only school I applied to, and, thankfully, I was accepted.

At Virginia State, I majored in political science and minored in French, having had a great foundation in French at Walker-Grant. The tuition was manageable for me as an in-state student. I received a $500 scholarship from a local businessman and a $300 scholarship from a local black social club. I supplemented the remainder of the tuition with loans from the National Bank of Fredericksburg (now PNC), which I repaid monthly after graduation until the loan was satisfied.

I had begun saving during my high school years, starting with my first job as a Head Start teacher's aide. I continued working during summer breaks, adding to my resume, a job as a clerk typist in the procurement section of the nearby army base Fort A.P. Hill (now Fort Walker). This, in effect, began my government service.

The Virginia State campus was beautiful, located high above the Appomattox River in Ettrick, Virginia (a suburb of Petersburg), pristinely landscaped with the fragrance of magnolias throughout. There was a mix of old, classically styled structures and newer more modern buildings that were added as its enrollment increased. I was very active and was elected as secretary-treasurer of the Student Government Association during my sophomore year. I played first-chair clarinet in the symphonic and marching band until my graduation four years later, and I sang in the choir for a short spell. I was very busy, but I was also a Dean's List student. At one point, I was even chosen Miss Virginia State College by popular vote of my fellow students.

Our symphonic band traveled each year, alternatively on a northern or southern tour, playing concerts in cities and communities along the way. We shared with our audiences a repertoire of classical and contemporary composers. These were magical evenings for us as performers and our very appreciative audiences.

During the football season our marching band, the Marching 110 (we had 110 members), not only excited our football fans but also fans at National Football League teams, such as the New York Giants, Philadelphia Eagles and Washington Commanders (formerly known as the Redskins, a name that was finally removed after years of controversy and objection by Indigenous communities and others). Virginia State was one of the first HBCU bands to be featured as halftime entertainment during nationally televised games; we never disappointed. Nobody went to get popcorn at halftime when *we* performed.

Life lessons from Dr. F. Nathaniel Gatlin, our band director extraordinaire, remained with me throughout my life: punctuality, practicing in the manner in which you were to perform, teamwork, and the like. He was a great influence on all of us. Many traits and actions I developed later as a leader were nurtured under his example. Dr. Gatlin's motto was "He who rests, rots." After Dr. Gatlin retired from Virginia State, he continued to conduct music and perform as an exceptional clarinetist. His last performance was conducting the Richmond Symphony, where he collapsed at the end of a performance and died doing what he loved.

My interest in international events was piqued at Virginia State. I developed my first serious interest in international affairs during my junior and senior years. The topic for my senior paper for the political science department chair, Dr. Sydney A. Reid, was *The Party System in Kenya*. Kenya received its independence in 1963 and was one of the few countries in Africa that had a two-party system at the time of independence. Most new African nations had been established under the strong arms of a single party, but Kenya was a little different: the people had organized two functioning parties. As a student of political science, I was fascinated by this somewhat different approach to self-government in Africa. I conducted research on the party system in Kenya, and my special interest in Kenya continued to grow as it moved forward in developing an independent nation-state.

My four years at Virginia State were exciting and fruitful. I was never homesick, nor did I find it onerous that freshman women could not visit home for the first six weeks. Not to mention that women were not allowed to wear trousers while shopping or browsing in downtown Petersburg. Our dean of women, Mrs. Maddox, was strict, poised, and her rules were to be adhered to without exception. Anyone who challenged or broke the rules, faced the consequences.

I joined Delta Sigma Theta Sorority, Inc. in 1967. I was inducted along with nine other women, all of us being Pyramid pledges. Service is the cornerstone of our sorority. While pledging Delta, I learned the importance of community service and empowering humankind, particularly the most vulnerable and underserved. I volunteered at the Central State facility for mentally ill patients – a real eye-opener that taught me about the challenges that persons with mental illness face and the paucity of resources available to help them.

The violent assassination of Reverend Dr. Martin Luther King, Jr., was a shocking moment in April of my senior year. My awareness of the need to continue fighting for social change and transformation was entrenched following Dr. King's murder. Many opportunities to continue his dream of justice for all were to follow in ways I could not have imagined.

Graduation from college came all too quickly. The four years at Virginia State were simply the best. The friendships, the academic preparation, and the leadership skills, all prepared me for what was ahead. I was excited and ready to hit the road. I was proud to return twice as the commencement speaker and an honorary doctorate.

CHAPTER 3

OH, SAY CAN UC?

F rom high above the Appomattox River, I headed to the Midwest and across the Ohio River. I applied for and received a Danforth Fellowship, suggested by the university placement office. The fellowship covered all tuition, books, lodging and a modest monthly stipend. While I was not at all certain what I wanted to do after graduation from Virginia State, I knew I wanted to pursue graduate studies to give me more time to decide, or as is often said, "find myself." Thus, I was soon off to the University of Cincinnati (UC) in Ohio, home to the Danforth Fellows program.

The contrasts were stark between the two campuses. I moved from VSU's old, colonial-style Byrd Hall (now renamed Otelia Howard Hall), where my freshman dorm room had been, offering neither elevator nor air-conditioning, to a beautiful, modern high-rise building on Scioto Street at UC. My new residence was one of several massive housing complexes that comprised the university's physical presence and formed part of that area's urban skyline. I lived on the ninth floor of Morgens Hall, one of the three towering high-rises on campus at the time. The stipend, though modest, was sufficient for food, some entertainment and a little travel. I learned to manage my money because that was all I was going to get. Many of the fellows chose to live off campus in nearby apartments with affordable rent. Some shared lodging. I chose to live on campus, which was somewhat more expensive, but I had two good reasons. I didn't have a car and I didn't know how to drive. Investing in a car at that time would have been another expense, and because Cincinnati winters can be rough, I wanted to be able to get to my classes and the library and not have to depend on public transportation or other means to get to campus.

My comfortable efficiency had everything I needed, including a small kitchen and a pull-out bed that doubled as a sofa by day. What a contrast this urban, massive campus in excess of ten thousand students was to the quiet, pristine bucolic campus of Virginia State! After a few days of adjusting to my new surroundings, things seemed quite normal. My biggest challenge was simply finding my way around the campus to locate the bookstore, dining areas, and the most direct ways to get to my classes on time. Once I conquered those challenges, I was well on my way. Being able to adjust quickly to new and different environments, to just pick up and go, seemed to come rather easy to me, and perhaps was a precursor of things to come.

Several other classmates from Virginia State also received the Danforth Fellowship, namely, Ron and Bessie Johnson and Betty Mitchell, so I had a small cohort of people

I knew at UC. I made many new friends, some of whom I maintain contact with today. Interestingly, one of them, a fellow political science major, Harvey Johnson, was to later become the first black mayor of Jackson, Mississippi. He was born in Vicksburg; before Harvey, I had never met anyone from Mississippi.

Our group of Danforth Fellows were all graduates of HBCUs. Harvey had attended Tennessee State University in Nashville. I shared stories about VSC with Harvey, and I learned about Tennessee State, Fisk and Meharry Medical College (all HBCUs in Nashville) from other Danforth Fellows. Naturally, Harvey mentioned Jefferson Street as being "that place" in Nashville, at the time. The exposure to students and professors from all parts of the U.S. and around the world was mesmerizing and exciting. That was an enriching and invaluable learning experience, quite different from any of my previous experiences. I adjusted well, and I enjoyed living in Cincinnati very much.

While in Cincinnati, I met two Jamaican students – one studying at UC and the other at Miami University of Oxford, Ohio. Clinton Hewan was a fellow political science major who later became a member of Jamaica's Foreign Service. Then there was Ruddy Brandon, who graduated from Miami University. He later became head of quality control at Estates Industries, Ltd., maker of Tia Maria, the famous Jamaican coffee liqueur. We all remained friends until their deaths.

I recall those days at UC and the limited finances I had. I didn't think I missed out on anything and don't think that now. While several of the other Danforth Fellows supplemented their finances by working part-time at the Opportunities Industrialization Centers founded by the renowned Dr. Leon Sullivan, I managed well with my stipend and was able to concentrate full-time on my studies.

The Jamaican students—and a few others with vehicles—were generous enough to give rides to me and other students as we went grocery shopping and had to climb the hill with grocery bags to get back to our housing. We also planned off-campus excursions and attended an Indianapolis 500, all of us riding in one small car and lodging at the home of a classmate whose family welcomed a bunch of hungry grad students. What a thrill! That would be my first and only time at the Indy 500. On another occasion, several of us piled into a small vehicle for a trip to New York City, the Big Apple, never minding the cramped car. The city was non-stop: Broadway, Times Square, Madison Square Garden, Yankee Stadium—something for everyone! Harlem may be my favorite because every time I visit there, I can't help but think of the great artists—Duke Ellington, Zora Neale Hurston, Langston Hughes, Paul Robeson, Ethel Waters and many others—who were the heartbeat and rhythm of the incomparable Harlem Renaissance. Even now, a trip to the Big Apple is always exciting!

There were thrilling times in Cincinnati as well, including getting to witness an occasional Cincinnati Royals basketball game and see the Big O, the great Oscar Robertson, work his magic on the court. We had so much fun at those games, including the unexpected thrill, after a game between the Milwaukee Bucks and Cincinnati Royals, of meeting Kareen Abdul Jabaar, then known as Lou Alcindor. From his seat on the team bus, he reached an unimaginably long arm across a throng of notepads and paper from autograph seekers and took my small slip of paper, as if he were grabbing a rebound, and wrote his name with the ease and perfection of his sky hook shot. What a surprise! I treasured that little piece of history until, after many years, it pretty much disintegrated. Today basketball—especially March Madness—remains my favorite spectator sport, although tennis is a close second.

A spiritual underpinning helped sustain me during both my matriculation at VSC and UC throughout the often-troubled waters I was yet to face. This was a direct result of the strong faith I had possessed since being baptized by my grandfather at eight years of age. Ongoing church attendance had also strengthened my faith. One of the other Danforth Fellows, Nancy Johnson, played the organ at Greater New Light Baptist Church, pastored by the civil rights icon The Reverend Dr. Fred L. Shuttlesworth. After she invited me to attend with her one Sunday, I joined the church and worshiped there regularly while at UC.

I decided to pursue a Master of Arts in political science at UC with a focus on international relations. UC professors provided strong foundations for what was to come. For my thesis, I decided to explore in depth the Kenyan party system. Having sufficient time, resources, and guidance opened the way to examine analytically the phenomenon that was Kenya at the time. My proposal was accepted by my committee after the first year of coursework. Next came the deep waters of tireless research. I successfully defended my thesis before a panel of three professors, and after making necessary edits and modifications, the construction of the Master of Arts bridge was almost complete.

The unrest and protests of the 1960s were taking place on campuses around the nation, including nearby Kent State University in Ohio, where some students who were protesting the war in Vietnam lost their lives. During this time, student activists also lost their lives on the campuses of Jackson State University in Mississippi and South Carolina State University, both HBCUs. Many campuses were closed nationwide just as the period of graduation began, as very few escaped the trauma of this period, including UC.

I did not receive my diploma from UC in a cap and gown; instead, the university mailed my diploma to me. It was just as precious as if I had marched down the aisle to the tune of Edward Elgar's "Pomp and Circumstance" to receive it.

How amazing it was to find that years after my graduation in 1970, the university invited me to deliver their annual commencement address to thousands of graduates. Someone in the Department of Alumni Affairs had certainly tracked my career since graduation. I flew into Cincinnati from Accra, Ghana, where I was serving as U.S. Ambassador. I marched in my cap and gown along with the president, faculty, students and dignitaries for this singular honor. The university conferred on me an honorary Doctor of Laws at the graduation ceremony, and I received VIP treatment during the graduation weekend that year.

The University of Cincinnati's president, Dr. Nancy L. Zimpher, poses with me in 2006 when I received an honorary Doctor of Laws degree and served as the commencement speaker.

CHAPTER 4

Professional/Paid Work Begins

For the time being, my academic pursuits had come to an end. It was time to find employment and begin to earn a living. This came in the form of three successive higher education teaching positions.

I was still in Cincinnati completing my degree when the call came from Voorhees College in Denmark, South Carolina. I had never heard of Voorhees, let alone Denmark, S.C., but each year, the small Episcopal church-affiliated school sent feelers to universities searching for newly minted graduates to fill expected faculty vacancies. The call came to me from the head of the Social Science Department, Dr. Bernard Cummings. I applied, was interviewed and was hired.

I taught bread-and-butter courses: U.S. government and a course in international relations. I cut my teaching teeth with students who were eager to learn, many of whom were older, mature matriculants and were former Vietnam veterans, older than my 23 years.

I had no high-rise apartment in a bustling metropolitan area in which to live. Instead, I lodged in the home of Joe and Mable Christian, faculty members at South Carolina State College (now University) in Orangeburg, S.C. They had extra rooms in their home which they rented to faculty at Voorhees. I had no vehicle, so I commuted to Denmark from Orangeburg, S.C., with a faculty member who had an automobile. The contrast between Cincinnati, Ohio, and Denmark, S.C. was stark and took quite a bit of adjustment. I did my best, but this job would be short lived.

Moving back east after one semester, I sought and found work at Bowie State College. The move was at the suggestion of Reverend A. Russell Awkard, a young pastor in my hometown whom I had dated after returning from Cincinnati and who, years later, would become my husband. Russell had suggested that I contact Bowie's administration for possible employment. Although I had never heard of Bowie State, Russell had grown up in Maryland, graduated from Howard University, and knew about many educational institutions in Maryland. Interviews with the Dean of Students and chair of the Political Science Department yielded a position at Bowie State. Maryland's oldest HBCU, it had been founded in Baltimore in 1865 to prepare educators for service in the state's schools.

I had to locate an apartment, learn to drive, and purchase a vehicle very quickly. I was needed for the upcoming semester. Thanks to Russell's knowledge of the area, I found an apartment in nearby Laurel, Maryland, a town also unknown to me. At the time, there was no public transportation to Bowie State, which was located in a suburban area outside Washington, D.C. Bowie State University, recently ranked as one of the top 20 HBCUs, now boasts a growing and thriving campus as well as competitive academic and championship athletic programs. The BSU campus now even has its own commuter train stop.

I had a chance to spread my wings and be both creative and expansive in my portfolio at Bowie State. My courses ranged from teaching early political theory (Thucydides and the Peloponnesian War) to Contemporary African politics. I also created the Political Science Department's first black politics course.

The black politics course was very popular. I combined theory with practice, invited practicing black political leaders to speak to the class, and co-taught the course with Maryland House of Delegates member Arthur A. King. Art King was a popular, activist/politician and respected civic leader. He rode a motorcycle to campus and had a charismatic personality. We combined theory and practice, using an innovative team-teaching approach, which proved to be a big hit with students.

Since we were so close to Washington, D.C., I invited and was successful in bringing to campus some important political figures, including Congresswoman Shirley Chisholm (first black woman to run for the U.S. presidency); numerous members of the U.S. Congressional Black Caucus, such as Congressmen Parren Mitchell, Charles Diggs, Louis Stokes, and John Conyers; and Walter E. Fauntroy (D.C.'s first non-voting delegate in the House). Marion Barry, then chair of the District of Columbia School Board and later a multi-term mayor, also was a guest lecturer.

I initiated a program in which students could receive academic credit for their studies abroad. Over the January term, students traveled to Haiti and Jamaica, where they attended classes at major universities, enjoyed cultural experiences, and made new friends.

I was selected as the faculty advisor to prepare a contingent of Bowie students to participate in the Model United Nations program held yearly in New York at U.N. headquarters. Bowie students were assigned to represent Ukraine.

While at Bowie State, I was one of the faculty selected to participate in the Thirteen College Curriculum Program (TCCP). TCCP was an innovative teaching methodology developed by the Institute for Services to Education (ISE), a Washington, D.C. organization. The program was called TCCP because 13 HBCUs initially agreed to use the curriculum materials for their freshman and sophomore core courses. ISE's research showed that TCCP students had higher rates of graduation than non TCCP curriculum students.

The objective was to get these students to complete the sophomore year, since statistics showed that after two years, they would more likely complete their four-year degree programs. ISE was led by its dynamic president, Dr. Elias

Blake, Jr., and deputies, Dr. Fredrick Humphries and Dr. Gerald L. (Jerry) Durley. Headquarters personnel believed I would be a good fit for their professional staff and extended an offer to work as a program associate. I accepted and moved on from Bowie State to the Institute's office on S Street in Northwest Washington, D.C.

My time at ISE was fascinating and intellectually challenging. I joined a team of outstanding and committed academic specialists from selected participating HBCUs. We developed and wrote materials for the textbooks used by the students participating in TCCP over six weeks at an intense summer conference. What an enriching and uplifting experience!

School Days Again

While working at ISE, I received information from the leadership that doctoral study grants were available. Jerry Durley encouraged me to apply, assuring me I'd be able to continue work and attend classes if accepted.

Always believing that learning is lifelong, and comfortable in academic environments as a student and professor, I decided to apply to the American University (AU) in D.C. I was accepted for doctoral studies in AU's School of International Service (SIS).

Although I was working full-time at ISE, the coursework for the doctoral program began in the evening, so I would be able to continue work while pursuing my studies. I thus began a two-year trek up and down Nebraska Avenue for evening classes, followed by a 45-minute drive in the dark of night back to Laurel, Maryland, usually arriving near midnight. In a few hours, at daybreak, it was time to drive back to NW Washington, to continue my important work at ISE the next morning.

Doctoral students at SIS were required to select three areas of focus to demonstrate comprehensive knowledge. I chose International Relations of Africa and International Communication. International Relations Theory was a requirement for all SIS students. After coursework was completed, I passed all three comprehensive exams, including International Communication with distinction. I thought I was now on my way to receiving a doctorate. My dissertation topic proposal was "African American Influences on U.S. Africa Foreign Policy." Little had been researched on the topic. My topic was approved, and I began my research.

While enrolled at AU, I became an active member of the National Conference of Black Political Scientists (NCOBPS) and also the American Political Science Association. I was so happy to know that there was a professional academic organization of African American political scientists that focused on political issues and research in my discipline. While attending some of the NCOPBS conferences, I met groundbreaking political scientists like Dr. Mae King, Dr. C. Vernon Gray, Dr. Leslie McLemore, and Dr. Haynes Walton, whose textbook I had used as a teacher. The gatherings were exciting, and I evidently made a positive impression on these individuals. Dr. Gray, who chaired the Political Science Department at Morgan State in Baltimore, indicated that he would like to interview me for a position, noting I would be the first woman to be hired in the section.

I was thrilled to be hired, not only at a larger university but also at another HBCU, this time in the city of Baltimore. I was living at the time in Landover, Maryland, and had the option to take Amtrak to avoid the drive. It was quite a different cohort of students after a four-year absence from teaching. I had to employ innovative techniques to capture their attention and engage them. My core courses were U.S. Foreign Policy, U.S. Government, and Contemporary African Politics. Were these signs of the diplomatic waters that I would soon encounter?

I had students from countries in Africa, and the Caribbean, as well as U.S.-born students all of whom were thirsty learners and made my teaching job exhilarating. I'm so proud of their professional achievements and have maintained contact with several of them. One of them, Dr. Max Hilaire, who became the chairman of the Department of Political Science at Morgan some years later, is a noted international lecturer, author, and Fulbright Scholar. Another of them, G. Anthony Hylton, graduated from Georgetown Law School, served as Foreign Minister and as Minister of Commerce and Industry in Jamaica and is an elected parliamentarian. Judge Sheila Thompson sits on the bench in Prince George's County, Maryland, and Yvette Taylor, a Georgetown Law graduate, has her own law firm specializing in elder legal advocacy. She is also an author and an elected official in Bucks County, Pennsylvania.

We remain in close contact. Some have reached out, seeking advice as they have navigated life's unsteady waters. Some I later invited for academic and cultural exchange programs as subject-matter experts or as bridge builders in countries where I served on diplomatic assignments.

CHAPTER 5

My Unexpected Diplomatic Path

E ven though I had pursued studies and received degrees in political science and related international-affairs disciplines, I wasn't familiar with U.S. Foreign Service career opportunities. As a college student, Department of State recruiters never visited my alma mater, HBCU Virginia State. But as fortune would have it, I had met Ambassador John Burroughs, a distinguished African American diplomat, through our mutual friend, Jerry Durley, while I was working at ISE.

Apparently, Ambassador Burroughs saw something in me that caused him to begin his personal recruitment effort. He told me I would do very well in the Foreign Service;

however, I was enjoying my teaching position as an assistant professor of political science at Morgan State University. I was happy molding young minds and expanding their horizons towards international engagement. I remained at Morgan.

Gradually, Ambassador Burroughs began to increase the pressure on me to pursue the U.S. Foreign Service. His diplomatic arguments and persistence finally won the day. I agreed to take a risk and dive into the unchartered waters of the U.S. Foreign Service. After successfully navigating the complexities of vetting for entering the Foreign Service and the associated bureaucratic hurdles, including extensive medical, security, and background checks, criminal, and as well as one's financial history (have you paid your taxes?), my diplomatic journey began.

I entered the new-officer orientation class, along with eighty-five other candidates; only five of us were African Americans. The entry officer training is entitled "A-100 -

Orientation to the Foreign Service." We learned the basics of the Foreign Service tradecraft required of new officers: consular, political, management, economic, and public diplomacy. After completing A-100 training, we all anxiously awaited notification of the presumably exotic places to which we would be assigned.

From the onset, my career did not follow the usual path. Surprisingly I wasn't sent overseas. Instead, I was assigned to the Department of State's Bureau of Intelligence and Research (INR), in Washington, D.C., where, perhaps because of my academic background, I served as an analyst. That two-year tour exposed me to the requirements of senior officials, including the Secretary of State, or "S" as we refer to that position.

I worked in the Office of Analysis for Africa (INR/AA). We prepared daily analyses for "S" in "the book," the compilation of daily morning briefing materials. We were also tasked with writing long-term analytical products. It was a wonderful learning experience that I would later draw upon on future overseas assignments.

Two of my long-term research analyses were entitled "South Africa–Zimbabwe Relations and The Buthelezi Factor in South Africa. " I would apply these same findings later while serving in a diplomatic position that may have been the most significant of my career for so many reasons. At that point, however, I never dreamed that I would spend six historic years in South Africa working on an assignment covering issues that I had written about on my first assignment as a new Foreign Service Officer (FSO).

CHAPTER 6

Bridgewater Goes to Brussels

My next assignment was to Brussels, Belgium. Few newly minted officers received overseas tours in European posts, but I did. Most are assigned as vice consuls in busy consular sections, or "visa mills" as we refer to them, due to the large number of visa applicants routinely processed.

I was thrilled to be located in the heart of Western Europe, convenient to all of the major capitals: Paris, London, Cologne. I could not wait to enjoy Michelin Star restaurants, Old World and amazingly delicious cuisine. My friends were already planning their visits!

I was assigned to a Junior Officer Rotational Program position (JORP), which meant that I would spend a year in the consular section and another year in the administrative section in the Joint Administrative Services section. As Junior Officer (JO), I was the supervisory officer in charge of embassy procurement, the large embassy motor pool, customs, shipping and travel. I also performed purchasing duties for a large post that included the U.S. Mission to the European Community and the U.S. Mission to the North Atlantic Treaty Organization (NATO). Loads of responsibilities for a first tour officer! Fortunately, we had a cadre of highly experienced locally employed Belgian staff who taught the—JOs now referred to as Entry Level Officers ELOs— the intricacies and details of these key portfolios since they had worked in those sections for many years.

Managing the large motor pool brought me to the first of the many troubled-water scenarios of my career. Unrest and the targeting of U.S. facilities and officials had become a common threat in Europe. The U.S. Department of State recognized the need to provide additional security to ambassadors and senior officers by armoring their official vehicles. My responsibility as procurement officer entailed interfacing with ANFO Motors, Europe, a Ford affiliate, to develop an armoring package not just for our vehicles in Brussels but for all of our European posts.

My knowledge of automobiles (then and now) was pretty basic: gasoline, tires and oil (GTO), but that would change in a hurry. I was learning techniques of armoring, visiting armoring facilities and coordinating with ANFO Motors' leadership in Brussels. Obtaining quotes for the armoring and clearing and obtaining approval from the Office of Diplomatic Security in Washington on the armoring specifications were some of the essential elements I had to traverse and conquer. I had to learn a completely new vocabulary relative to vehicles and armoring requirements.

The big day came when I had to meet with the senior officials of ANFO Motors in Cologne, Germany. They were the technical and armoring specialists and the financial officers with whom I had discussed our requirements. I was the sole U.S. officer and only woman in the room at a long table of men, most of whom were smoking cigarettes heavily. Fortunately, the local ANFO Motors Brussels contact, Marc Vandersmissen, who had been my major interlocutor during the negotiating process, was in the room, so his familiar face and confidence in me were a great comfort.

I took a deep breath and began to speak. I began by carefully explaining how thick the bullet resistance of the windows had to be and our requirements for the armoring of the doors. I had to make it clear how critically important it was to secure armored vehicles for our chiefs of mission expeditiously, while meeting exact specifications and negotiating to get the best price. I made the case, fielded questions convincingly-and the armoring process began!

Those were indeed troubled waters that I bridged successfully and effectively. I surprised myself, but despite being a rookie, if you will, and a bit uneasy, leading that meeting seemed natural for me. I couldn't help but think back to my childhood days in Fredericksburg and remembered Mrs. Todd's description of me as "diplomatic." On my way back to Brussels, I was excited to share my relief with my dear friend Christine Johnson, who was visiting me in Brussels and had accompanied me to Cologne, enjoying Cologne as a tourist while I worked.

During my year in the embassy's management section, I became the embassy "expert" in organizing and managing high-level visits. Embassy Brussels would welcome two visits yearly by the Secretaries of State and Defense, and other senior officials to participate in NATO and other security planning commission meetings with our key allies.

With three U.S. missions in Brussels—the U.S. bilateral mission—U.S. Embassy—the U.S. Mission to the European

Commission—and the U.S. Mission to the North Atlantic Treaty Organization—VIPs and official visitors coming to Brussels for meetings or transiting Brussels routinely required Embassy Brussels' management support.

It was while managing the motor pool that I had my first experience in coordinating with the U.S. Secret Service. Former President Jimmy Carter was visiting Brussels to give a speech. Naturally, our embassy was charged with meeting, assisting, and providing transportation and other support as might be requested. I met my first Secret Service Agents during President Carter's visit. The advance chief, who went by the name "Buster," was based in Atlanta and a well-known member of the Carter detail. Secret Service requirements are exact, and we followed them to the letter, coordinating all the while with local Belgian security officials.

I will always remember the ride from the airport after greeting President Carter. After welcoming President Carter at the military airbase, the official party was directed to the vehicles lined on the tarmac for the motorcade escort into Brussels. President Carter and the Secret Service were in an armored Belgian Maserati; I was in a Ford Sedan as we went flying through tunnels into the city with a Secret Service advance agent. I thought to myself that if I survived, I would certainly be fine in the Foreign Service.

I worked with the U.S. Secret Service again when Vice President George Herbert Walker Bush visited Brussels. I had gotten my feet wet with President Carter's visit and felt confident with subsequent high-level visitors. The head of the vice-presidential Secret Service detail was Agent Hubert Bell, the first African American Secret Service agent that I had encountered. He was extremely helpful in explaining the additional requirements for a sitting president or vice president as opposed to a former official.

Hubert and I learned that we had something in common: I had worked with his brother Joe Bell, who worked with the Head Start Program at Howard University during the time I was working at Bowie State. Hubert and I remained friends as my career blossomed. The small number of African Americans that were in senior positions of responsibility in the U.S. had few layers of separation. In our sidebar conversations, we usually found we knew someone in common or had shared similar experiences in our formative professional years.

The Brussels management section had created a time-tested template for how high-level visits and motorcade movements were to be managed. I mastered the art, and our team executed the visits flawlessly.

I rotated to the consular section after a year in management. I spent six months in the American Citizen Services section and six months on the visa line. My reputation for handling high-level visits was stellar. Management called on me frequently from my consular duties to handle logistics and motorcades for other important visits. The year I spent as vice consul would be the only consular work I performed until I became consul general in Durban, South Africa. The fundamentals and practical experience in Brussels served me well throughout the remainder of my career whenever consular issues arose.

Dining in Brussels was an art form; the choices were endless. You could get an amazing meal at one of the numerous neighborhood restaurants or at a 4-star Michelin establishment. My first degustation was a 12-course culinary tasting journey that I prayed would never end. Each new course of chef specialties was more delectable than the previous.

Desserts made fresh daily in the pastry shops were unmatched, except of course by the Belgian chocolates, Godiva being the most well-known, although Leonidas chocolates were my favorite. I didn't discriminate, however, and tasted all of them over the course of my tour. In fact, I was the lucky beneficiary of gift boxes of chocolates throughout my tour of duty.

Eating Belgian frites (French fries), twice cooked with their most delicious mayonnaise, forever ended my use of ketchup. I also think I had tastings of more than a fair share of the over three hundred Belgian beers. My favorite was Le Fruit Defendu (or Forbidden Fruit), and a few other Trappist brews.

I departed Brussels a more seasoned and cosmopolitan person, having traveled extensively throughout Belgium and much of Europe. I had the rich experience of visiting London, Paris, Vienna, Rome, Amsterdam, many of them just an easy, comfortable train ride away. I recall listening to the Blue Danube Waltz while sailing on the Danube River, and I attended my first opera at the world-famous Vienna Opera House, where later that evening, I stumbled upon my first (but not my last) Sacher Torte dessert, an Austrian chocolate cake with a wonderful blend of apricot jam and a chocolate glaze. It is still my favorite today.

The many driving trips to Paris for weekend getaways were also a treat. I visited all of the famous points of interest, enjoyed French cuisine and absorbed the sights, sounds and smells of Paris, the City of Lights. I soon realized why the French term, La Belle France, meaning "the beautiful one," is used as a metaphor to describe the country's beauty and style.

Several of my friends, classmates and former teachers visited me in Brussels. My mother, grandmother and Aunt Lois were among the guests. They were all great hits with my Belgian colleagues and Foreign Service friends. All of my visitors were able to travel to neighboring countries as well, enjoying the sighs and warm hospitality.

My assignment as a Junior Officer also exposed me to a world of career-enhancing Foreign Service experiences, which included leading and managing diverse teams, interacting with interagency partners, and valuing and utilizing my strengths and unique talents. I drew upon these learning experiences as my career evolved. I often reflect on my belief that my management experience in Brussels exposed me to all the critical elements of an embassy and what it takes to run a smooth, effective, and productive mission.

CHAPTER 7

More Training Days

F ollowing my Brussels tour, I was selected to attend the Mid-Level Training Program at the Foreign Service Institute. The Department of State identifies officers at the midpoint of their careers for further training in preparation for assignments of more responsibility and authority. After six months in mid-level training, it was time for my next assignment. I had been assigned to Kingston, Jamaica, as a political officer with a focus on labor issues.

In preparation for my assignment, I was chosen as one of two Department of State officers to attend the Harvard University Trade Union Program. The six-month-long program in Cambridge, Massachusetts, prepared labor officers to perform the labor officer function effectively. We had lectures from top labor leaders and theorists from the U.S. government and private sectors. One such lecturer was the distinguished former Secretary of Labor John Dunlop. The basics of negotiating, collective bargaining and mediation were to come in very handy in my work in Jamaica. Our classmates were practicing trade union members and union officials, and we Foreign Service Officers learned much from their practical experiences.

Within days of my arrival in Kingston, Jamaica, the country was in the throes of a nationwide general strike. I reported to Washington the details of the strike, having attended a large rally to hear firsthand from local labor leaders the issues of concern. That cable was but one of many I sent to Washington covering the active trade union movement in Jamaica.

Jamaica historically had a very robust and vocal trade union movement which played a seminal role in the development of the political process over the years. The two major trade unions, the Bustamante Industrial Trade Union and the National Workers Union were aligned respectively with the two major political parties – the Jamaica Labor Party of Alexander Bustamante and the Norman Manley-led People's National Party. Bustamante and Manley each become prime minister for a time, leading the country in the early periods of independence.

My assignment also entailed covering the People's National Party, which was then the opposition party. Numerous trade union personalities with whom I engaged later became leaders in their respective political parties. They remembered me on my return years later as the U.S. ambassador. The relationships and professional friendships that I developed during this tour of duty helped establish my capabilities as a bona fide, honest, fair, and trusted broker. These relationships were forged amid the troubled waters of strikes and political unrest, during which, on behalf of the U.S., I was able to provide training, technical assistance and educational materials for union members.

When that tour of duty in Kingston ended, I returned to Washington for an assignment in the Bureau of Oceans and International Environmental and Scientific Affairs (OES). Ambassador John Negroponte was then serving as the Assistant Secretary. Andrew Parker, with whom I had served in Jamaica was Ambassador Negroponte's special assistant. Andy phoned me to say he believed I'd be a good fit for a position in OES as the Deputy Coordinator for Population Issues, assisting Ambassador Nancy Ostrander, who served as Coordinator.

After speaking with Ambassador Ostrander and learning more about job requirements, I thought, why not? I'll get an opportunity to work with Ambassador Negroponte, a distinguished career diplomat (years later named Director of National Intelligence), learn new tradecraft, travel, and contribute to our efforts at managing fast population growth in key areas around the globe. I added the OES position on my list of possible next assignments, and I was selected.

Working on this portfolio entailed extensive travel to countries with rapid population growth. I went on official visits to Thailand, Egypt, El Salvador, Honduras, Turkey, Guatemala, and Mexico to meet with family planning and legislative officials in those countries. My mandate was to encourage governments to provide resources for women to plan the size of their families and improve maternal and child health through legislation.

After my assignment in OES, I accepted a brief assignment as an analyst in the Office of the Geographer, tracking worldwide international labor trends and analyzing the political and economic implications for the U.S. I always enjoyed analytical work and was happy to return to the Bureau of Intelligence and Research, where I had first served as a Foreign Service Officer.

CHAPTER 8

Marching to Pretoria

Pamela Bridgewater's role as the first African American woman political officer posted at the U.S. Embassy in Pretoria in 1990 and her role as Consul General in Durban in 1993 were well known. I was extremely proud of the work she was engaged in to help end the Apartheid system and to support President Nelson Mandela.

—Ambassador Makila James

My assignment in the Office of the Geographer was brief. Ambassador John Burroughs again sought me out. He had served as ambassador to Malawi, as well as consul general in Cape Town, South Africa. John said to me, "You know, there's a political officer job open in South Africa you should bid on." I said, "I don't think so." I reminded

John that I grew up in segregated Virginia, and I did not relish experiencing more racial separation under apartheid. He informed me that Ambassador William Lacy Swing, our ambassador in South Africa, supported my being assigned to Pretoria (South Africa) when the position opened up. Ambassador Swing was a highly distinguished diplomat with a stellar career and reputation. I would be the only black officer in the entire very large political section.

I'm not sure why I changed my mind; perhaps the proven diplomatic and persuasive skills of Ambassador Burroughs and the chance to work with Ambassador Swing, but I decided to add Pretoria to my wish list of assignments. Perhaps it was the proven diplomatic and persuasive skills of Ambassador Burroughs or the chance to work with Ambassador Swing. But despite Pretoria being the bastion of apartheid and Afrikaner white privilege, I updated my onward assignment wish list to include the political officer position at the U.S. embassy in Pretoria.

Mother Knows Best?

When I informed my mother that I had listed Pretoria, South Africa, as a potential next assignment, she initially thought she misheard me. When she realized I was serious, she called out, "My daughter has just lost it now!" That reaction was in large part because she was concerned for my well-being as a product of segregation. Stories in the U.S. media about difficult days in South Africa made her fear the possibility of my working as a black American diplomat in a possibly hostile environment.

My former Morgan State student Yvette Taylor asked, "If you get sick, what are you going to do? Who's going to take care of you? Will you be able to go to the hospitals in Pretoria?" My family and friends worried about those kinds of things, but none of that ever crossed my mind. I simply presumed that if I were sent there, somebody was going to take care of me.

I soon received the news that I had been assigned to Pretoria. Apartheid was still in effect as I prepared to head to the extremely turbulent waters of South Africa.

In preparation for this assignment, I enrolled in the area studies curriculum for southern Africa at the Foreign Service Institute, now renamed the George P. Schultz National Foreign Affairs Training Center, located in Arlington, Virginia. Area studies training provides information and background on the region and the specific country to which one is assigned.

Upon completion of the course, I paid courtesy calls on Department of State and Africa Bureau officers who would be tracking South Africa in Washington. That could easily have been every office and agency. All eyes were on South Africa, a country that was either on the brink of a peaceful transition from apartheid or about to erupt into unthinkable violence.

When I met with the Assistant Secretary for Africa, Ambassador Jeff Davidow, he admonished me to "go on out there to Pretoria and do your job. I know you're going to do your job well, but remember to have fun, and don't take yourself too seriously." I remembered those words throughout my career and gave the same advice to other officers as well as to colleagues. You should never take yourself too seriously but *always* take your job seriously. A healthy work–life balance is ideal but often hard to maintain, requiring one to juggle the often-competing demands of diplomatic work and family responsibilities. The most successful officers were those who were able to strike a balance between work and family, and that was important to me.

Around the time I was preparing for my assignment, black U.S. law-makers were developing a keen interest in South Africa. The U.S. Congressional Black Caucus (CBC) had commissioned two sculptures, one for South African hero, Mr. Nelson Mandela, and the other for his wife Winnie.

Although the CBC had been unable to schedule a time to present the artwork during Mr. Mandela's hectic 1990 U.S. thank-you tour, when members of the Caucus learned that I had been assigned to the U.S. Embassy in Pretoria, they contacted me, asking if I would take the two sculptures to South Africa and deliver them to Mr. Mandela on behalf of the Caucus. I'm sure they considered this to be a great opportunity for a young black diplomat to meet the international icon, Nelson Mandela.

The sculptor was African American Ed Dwight, who also happened to be the first black astronaut chosen by President John F. Kennedy for the NASA manned space program. Mr. Dwight was never selected to go into space and withdrew from NASA due to controversial racial backlash within the space program that had prevented him from advancing. While Dwight did not reach outer space as an astronaut, he embarked on another career that took him to new heights as a world-renowned and acclaimed sculptor. At age

90, Ed Dwight finally made a trip aboard the Space X spacecraft that carried private citizens into space. How thrilling that Dwight finally realized his earlier ambition, getting his day in space at long last!

The CBC representative delivered the sculptures to me in a huge black steamer trunk at my Landover, Maryland, home. I imagined the trunk was so large because of the abundant layers of packing materials required to safeguard the art during the long trip to South Africa.

I decided to break up the more than 20 hours trip to Pretoria with a stop in Brussels, where I had served earlier in my career and still had friends. I arranged for a large vehicle to meet me at the Brussels airport in order to safeguard the trunk during my stopover. I didn't want to let the precious cargo out of my sight.

After an enjoyable visit with Belgian friends and former U.S. colleague Diane Hernandez, dining on my favorite Belgian dishes, I headed back to the airport in Zaventem, just outside Brussels, to continue my journey to Pretoria. This airport was built for the 1958 World Exhibition and was a wonderful hub for jumbo jets and cargo.

At check-in, the agent indicated I would need to pay more than $800 for excess baggage. I nearly fainted, having minimal cash on hand. Thankfully, I had not left home without my American Express card. No way I was leaving Brussels without that trunk!

I landed in Johannesburg, South Africa, in August 1990 at the Jan Smuts International Airport. Smuts had been the chief architect of apartheid. The airport was later renamed for Oliver R. Tambo, who had been president of the African National Congress during Mandela's imprisonment. Tambo and Mandela had been lifelong friends, beginning when, as young attorneys, they had served together as law partners

It was the dry season and the terrain was brown and bleak. I hoped that wasn't a sign of how my tour of duty would be. A thousand thoughts filled my mind, and a fair amount of trepidation crept in. I asked myself if I had made the correct decision and how I would fare in this environment.

My uncertainty and anxiety didn't last long. I made my way through the South African Immigration window and on to Customs after collecting my checked luggage. A Customs officer with a thick Afrikaner accent asked brusquely, "What is in the trunk?" I replied that it contained personal items—well, they were! The trunk was entrusted to me. It was mine at the time. I silently prayed, *"Please don't let them confiscate this trunk. Please don't let it get lost on my watch!"* And it did not. Fortunately, traveling with a United States Diplomatic Passport was surely some help in moving through Customs.

Each new officer assigned to our diplomatic posts is given a "sponsor." Sponsors ensure that there are food staples at our assigned housing, some local currency and other necessities to get started. I had informed my embassy sponsor that I had a huge steamer trunk and needed a vehicle large enough to transport me from the airport with the treasured items. I was very happy that I had also connected with Judy Marvin, the senior supervisory General Services Officer who managed the motor pool vehicles as one of her responsibilities. Judy and I had worked together in Jamaica on my first assignment there (1985–87).

The U.S. embassy was in an office building complex on Pretorius Street in the heart of downtown Pretoria. The complex was also the headquarters of the South African Police Department! I wondered whether I should be comforted or concerned by this. I had no time to worry, though, for my work duties began immediately. I scheduled introductory courtesy calls on the ambassador and deputy chief of mission and informed the ambassador's able assistant, Jane Jgzynka, about the artwork. Jane quickly secured a meeting with Mr. Mandela so that he might receive the artwork.

Ambassador Swing included me in the delegation to present the sculptures to Mandela, reminding the other officers that there would have been no artwork without me. We were off to ANC headquarters on busy Sauer Street in Johannesburg for the 40-minute drive from Pretoria to deliver the artwork. What a moment! Being introduced to Nelson Mandela—a man larger than life—I remembered to breath, but just barely!

When I first met him, many things stood out – first of all, his handshake. For an elderly man, his handshake was strong and firm. Not only had he been a boxer, but he had big hands. Sometimes he would shake my hand so tightly that I felt intense pressure on my ring finger, and it was painful. Of course, I didn't flinch or say "Ouch, that hurts!" I just thought, "S*queeze my poor little finger for as long as you want sir!"* That was the diplomatic way.

Our presentation of the art pieces was covered in the local papers (including a photo). The sculpture for Mr.

Mandela was entitled "Song of Freedom"; Winnie Mandela's sculpture was named "Masai Woman."

This photograph was taken in 1990 during the presentation of the two sculptures by Ed Dwight, being gifted to Nelson and Winnie Mandela. The sculptures are visible on a table in the foreground.

From that moment on, a special rapport developed between Mr. Mandela and myself. I'm not sure why, but many observers said to me that I resembled a young Winnie. I wasn't sure that that was the case, but thereafter I developed unprecedented access to Mr. Mandela and his trusted staff. His special assistants and closest personal staff were Jessie Duarte and Barbara Masekela, both of whom later became

South Africa's ambassadors to Cuba and the United States respectively.

This photograph, taken in 1990, shows from left, Ms. Jessie Duarte (in background), assistant to Nelson Mandela; Pamela Bridgewater; Marshall McCallie, deputy chief of mission; Ambassador William L. Swing; and Nelson Mandela.

Ambassador Swing routinely turned to me when he wanted to schedule appointments with Mr. Mandela for himself or other senior U.S. officials, who flooded South Africa as the transition was unfolding. My portfolio included black politics. Yes, the U.S. embassy political section had divided our work portfolios into either "black" or "white" politics. I thought it strange. I wondered why we weren't assigned to either "liberation groups" or "non-liberation groups" or perhaps assigned to either "governmental groups" or "non-governmental groups." It seemed to me that our embassy, like South Africa itself, needed to evolve in its ways of thinking.

I was also responsible for assessing political developments in several of the "homelands." I often traveled to Bophuthatswana (Bop), where Tswana-speaking people were designated and forced to live. I covered Venda, home of the Venda people, as well as Transkei, where Xhosa-speaking people lived. Nelson Mandela had been born in Transkei.

The largest African group, the Zulus, mostly resided in the province of Natal, where I later served. Each homeland had its own "government" and legislative structures. Collectively, they were called Bantustans, a name created by the apartheid state to separate the races. The governing powers did not want blacks to be integrated nor to be a part of the aggregate nation.

I vividly remember covering the trial of a young ANC human rights activist, named Patrick Huma, living in Bop who had been arrested for fomenting political unrest. He was pencil-thin and accused by the homeland government of stimulating political unrest.

I traveled frequently from Pretoria to Bop as we called it (shortening the name) to cover his trial. Mr. Huma was subsequently acquitted and upon the formation of a nonracial government, he was later elected to the national Parliament! My presence at his trial every day was an important virtual bridge that very likely contributed to his being acquitted, knowing the eyes of the U.S. were watching and reporting what was transpiring.

One of our most important sections of the U.S. embassy was a cohort of officers who worked closely with South African counterparts to draft a new constitution. Several members of the U.S. team had been assigned to Pretoria by the Office of the Legal Advisor at the Department of State.

This was an intense process. The U.S. was convinced not only that a peaceful transition from apartheid was possible but also that the changes needed to dismantle apartheid were forth coming. We were committed to assisting South Africans in their preparation for change.

The embassy's budget had considerable resources that we could use to anticipate and support future developments. For example, I was asked to manage a $500,000 self-help program, designed to benefit all areas of the country, including the so-called homelands, by awarding small grants to start businesses and improve economic conditions.

State Department staff had identified many issues of critical importance, chief among them being South Africa's constitutional dispensation. We also sought, however, to make effective use of the department's International Visitor Program (IVP). Pretoria was allotted as many as fifty international visitors per yearly cycle, and our embassy officers had a great track record, nominating key individuals for the

IVP who later became leaders in every critical aspect of South African life.

Our instincts were correct. On March 17, 1992, President F. W. DeKlerk called a referendum on whether to move ahead with transitioning from apartheid. He hoped that a vote in favor would give him the mandate and enhanced public support to continue the effort to dismantle apartheid that he had already begun. The vote was "yes," but troubling events were occurring around the townships.

Black South Africans from the townships were being hacked and slaughtered aboard commuter trains as they rode to work in Pretoria or Johannesburg. The details were frightening. Some people saw these brutal killings as random acts of violence, but Mandela asserted that a Third Force was responsible.

It was a dark and ugly time. Proof eventually emerged, showing the unrest had indeed been fomented by Afrikaner nationalists and sympathizers, with complicity by certain elements within the police forces. While the U.S. embassy team remained hopeful and fully engaged throughout this cycle of violence, we accepted that there would be setbacks. Our mission never lost hope that the transition to a nonracial government could become a reality.

I could and did find common ground with all the groups with whom I interacted, which became a hallmark of my diplomatic work. During my time in Pretoria, I accepted an invitation from Afrikaner contacts to attend a rugby game at Loftus Versfeld. Rugby was considered the sport of the Afrikaners and the whites. I was the only black person there who was not in a subservient role. It was fine because it was an opportunity to learn rugby.

I later attended South Africa's World Cup championship game, which they won to the delight of blacks and whites. It was not just a win for rugby but a victory for the new rainbow nation, exhibited by the thunderous applause pulsating throughout the stadium. I also witnessed the infamous tip of the cap Mr. Mandela gave to the crowd, standing tall and confident, next to rugby team captain, Francois Pienaar, wearing a jersey of the Springboks, the national rugby team. It was indeed magical, and I was there, recording this history in my mind! This was the stuff of which movies are made, and many accounts of this period were in fact made into cinematic productions for the big screen.

Unafraid

I was never unduly fearful, although these were terrifying times. We all exercised prudence, but I don't recall being afraid, perhaps because I never took unnecessary risks or more likely since that was just the way I've always been. I think the only time I may have felt a little unnerved (and I think anyone in their right mind probably would have been) was in the aftermath of the assassination of a very popular South African personality, ANC and Communist party member, Chris Hani.

After Hani was assassinated, Mr. Mandela addressed the nation on national television and called for peace. He told the nation, "Just as some crazed white person assassinated Hani as he retrieved his Sunday newspaper at his suburban Johannesburg home, it was also a white Afrikaner neighbor who got the license plate of the person fleeing his home, enabling the police to later apprehend this perpetrator." Sharp anger prevailed among the African communities. However, those troubled, boiling waters were calmed by Mandela's forceful, calm presidential-sounding message and presence, calling for peace and understanding, which helped settle a restive nation in this critical moment.

Shaking hands with Nelson Mandela in Durban
Photo by D. Michael Cheers, Ebony Magazine

By the time of Hani's assassination, I had transferred to a new assignment in Durban. I received a call from the embassy's regional security officer (RSO) in Pretoria asking for "my assessment" of the potential security threat as massive plans were being made for Hani's funeral at a large stadium in Johannesburg. He wanted to know what I thought about our school children and whether I thought they should be allowed to go to their American school, located outside Johannesburg and on the route to where the funeral was to be held.

I had maintained regular communication with my contacts in the ANC, PAC and AZAPO after leaving Pretoria. I informed the RSO that the school children and ambassador's party should not face unrest that would prevent them from going to school or attending the funeral; however, I advised him that the school children should take an alternate route as a precautionary measure.

Ambassador Lyman, his wife Helen, and the RSO received bulletproof vests for the trip to the funeral. I did not receive one, although I rode to the funeral with the ambassador as part of the official U.S. delegation. I thought, well, if any bullets start flying, I guess I'm the lowest on the totem pole. If there were bullets and one strayed, I thought it would get me. Nevertheless, I had answered the call to duty to face the uncertainty of the funeral day. Although waves of unsettled water seemed to be swirling all around me, I didn't think twice about traveling to Pretoria for the funeral: duty called.

Nearing the stadium on the outskirts of Johannesburg where the funeral was to take place, our entourage encountered angry youth on the side of the highway. When we heard and felt our vehicle being hit, I wasn't certain what was striking us, though the sounds were menacing. The pelting could have been bullets. Then it appeared that rocks and large stones were the weapons protesters were hurling at many of the passing vehicles, and we were not solely being targeted. Nevertheless, this was the closest I had yet come to personal danger.

The Killing Fields of Natal

As my three-year assignment in Pretoria was coming to an end, I began thinking about my next tour of duty. Ambassador Johnny Young had been assigned to the Department of

State in the Bureau of Human Resources (Personnel Department). I was on leave and stopped by the Department of State, as it is often common practice to visit with career counselors to discuss onward assignments. During my visit at Ambassador Young's office, he informed me about a job that "might just be good for you." Someone had been scheduled to go to South Africa as the Principal Officer (Consul General) in the Durban office, but the assignment had been broken. So the position was open. "It's a two-grade stretch," Ambassador Young told me, meaning that it was two grades higher than my rank at the time, "but I think you can do the job. In fact, I know you can."

I added Durban to the list of choices for my next assignment and had the strong support of Ambassador Lyman. Ambassador Young said Ambassador Lyman would have to inform the department of his support for my assignment to Durban. Ambassador Lyman's cable supporting my assignment came immediately. I soon received official word that I had indeed been assigned to Durban. The troubled waters that flooded the landscape of KwaZulu in Natal province would be my home base for three more years.

After I informed Mr. Mandela that I would be completing my tour in Pretoria, he said, "I hear you are leaving us in Pretoria. You know that is going to make me very sad, but I know you are going to Durban to do a good job, and a job that needs to be done."

Durban is the smallest of the three South African based U.S. Consulates General; Johannesburg and Cape Town are the other two. In many ways, Durban was the most consequential during those days. We had only two American officers but a huge workload. I was the first black woman to serve as consul general. My first speech was to the Jewish community of Durban, which I delivered at the main synagogue.

Consulate General Durban had administrative responsibility for clearing and processing household effects that arrived in the Port of Durban for all our embassies in southern Africa. Our small, dedicated, and highly competent contingent of South African nationals also processed non-immigrant visas, American citizens services, and passports and provided information on immigrant visas for processing in Pretoria. Their immediate supervisor was Vice Consul Baxter Hunt, who managed the section superbly. He was succeeded by Scott Hamilton. Our hard-working team was kept busy amid turbulent waters of ongoing violence and unrest that occupied our minds and flooded our landscape.

Finding ways to bring the warring groups together and help restore peace and stability were priorities for the U.S. My personal security was zero. I had a local unarmed driver, and when he was off duty, I drove myself. When I assumed duty in Durban, our consulate did not even have a metal detector in a country where armed weapons were permitted to be carried openly, and the political landscape was fraught with instability and uncertainty. I recognized at once that this was a vulnerability for our staff, who faced the public daily. I requested a security assessment of our facility from the RSO in Pretoria, which resulted in our consulate receiving a magnetometer and some additional security enhancements. I was grateful for even these minimal improvements. We pressed on.

I traveled the whole of the province, engaging all the groups, the South Africans, those of Indian origin, English speakers, white Afrikaners, and of course the Zulu population—South Africa's largest ethnic group.

Dr. Mangosuthu Buthelezi was the head of the KwaZulu homeland and president of the Inkatha Freedom Party (IFP). He was my principal interlocutor in Durban. Numerous congressional delegations came to South Africa to talk with him, encouraging him to participate in the elections that had been scheduled following DeKlerk's referendum on moving ahead with a transition.

Photo of Chief Mangosuthu Buthelezi, Member of Parliament, and Ambassador Pamela Bridgewater on a return visit to Durban, 2020.

Buthelezi said Inkatha (IFP) would boycott the all-race election that had finally been negotiated and agreed upon, causing many to worry that the largest ethnic group in the country would not participate in these seminal elections. I attended countless meetings with Chief Buthelezi and provincial officials such as, Dr. Frank Mdlalose, chairman of the IFP. I arranged meetings with U.S. officials such as Congressman Donald Payne, Congressman Dennis De Concini and numerous others who came in to try to persuade Buthelezi to participate. Buthelezi insisted that official visitors, including Ambassador Lyman, travel three hours from Durban to Ulundi, the capital of Zululand, to meet with him. Only if the Inkatha leader already had an event in Durban or Johannesburg could any meetings be scheduled in those locations.

With election preparations in high gear, Washington policymakers had an insatiable thirst for information. They feared that the ongoing violence—along with the boycott announced by Buthelezi—would end up derailing the scheduled election.

I drafted most of the political reports and was nominated for the director general's reporting award by Pretoria's Political Chief John Campbell. Washington policymakers had an intense interest in whether Inkatha would participate—and if so, how.

Natal was the country's most violent province. The Zulus supporting the ANC and the Zulus supporting the Inkatha

Freedom Party often attacked each other in incredibly brutal ways: brother against brother, father against son. The area was referred to as the "Killing Fields of Natal," as the killings were intense, unrelenting and bloody.

I decided to investigate the ongoing violence in these areas. I wanted to examine the situation up-close to determine its root causes and to seek solutions from those intimately involved in the trouble spots.

I delegated Vice Consul Hunt the responsibility to write one of the cables. Our reports were dispatched not just to the Department of State but to all of the South Africa watchers across myriad U.S. agencies. The State Department described the reporting from Durban as 'riveting.'

The date of the first nonracial election had been set for April 27, 1994. Although Buthelezi and Inkatha were still holdouts, excitement was bubbling over, both in South Africa as well as worldwide. Several religious and community leaders called for a peace conference amongst the local players in Natal. I was invited to speak -- the only non-South African asked to participate in that event. It was a time for me to do what has always come naturally to me. On that slightly overcast day, I knew it was important that I speak about ways to calm the waters, making clear why violence must be quelled. When I left the podium, it seemed—at least to my diplomatic mind—that the clouds had given way: the rest of that day was bright and sunny.

Five days before the scheduled elections, Buthelezi agreed to participate. Because the ballots had already been printed, Buthelezi's name and party logo could be added only as the last option on an otherwise alphabetized list.

A Witness to History

I served as an official election observer and had to undergo the same training as all election observers, local and international. All the members of my small staff were deployed at different places. I had received permission to go to the polling place at Ohlange High School, just outside

Durban, where Mr. Mandela would vote—the most unforgettable part of election day for me. I awakened at around 4 a.m. Soon my trainer came, and I completed my exercises to start this momentous day. I had invited my housekeeper, Thulile Shoba, to accompany me. After all, her country stood on the brink of making history. I figured that if anyone should be present at this notable time, it was her.

Mandela arrived at the polling station with eyes, lights and cameras from around the world jockeying for position. When his car stopped at the polling site, he was accompanied by his regular security officers, whom I knew well. He confidently got out of his vehicle and smiled broadly, as only he could.

The sophisticated cameras from around the world outclassed my small digital camera. I also had a clear and unobstructed vantage point. But then, amid the excitement as Mr. Mandela headed into the voting location, I nearly forgot to click the button on my camera!

The last-second photograph taken by Pamela Bridgewater as Nelson Mandela headed into his voting location during the historic 1994 election.

He exited shortly thereafter to thunderous applause heard around the world, waved his raised arms as only Mandela could do, and returned to his vehicle. I pinched myself as to the reality of what I had witnessed—a moment never to be forgotten, forever cherished.

Shortly thereafter, I assumed my duty-station at the Durban City Hall polling station, where I continued my observation of the Durbanites voting peacefully. The lines were long and winding. The atmosphere among the voters standing patiently in lengthy lines was electric. Women stood under parasols to shield themselves from the hot sun. Black and white voters chatted like old friends. It was wonderful.

Throughout the day, Vice Consul Baxter Hunt and I returned periodically to the consulate to send reports to Washington, which was anxiously awaiting real-time reports assessing how voting was proceeding. I had taken a flight earlier with the police to view some of the polling sites. Despite the euphoria of election day, the Natal landscape remained fluid and unpredictable, but my close connection with the police spokesman, Colonel Bala Naidu, enabled me to have accurate, firsthand information on security and related matters without either me or my staff taking unnecessary risks.

The historic day passed largely without incident. Although someone had tried to use an explosive to deter people from voting, South Africans came out in massive numbers to cast their votes. The ANC won, having received an over-whelming number of votes.

Chris Saunders, the white South African business mag-nate and head of Tongaat Hulett Sugar Company in Durban, told me that he hosted Mandela for dinner the evening before the elections. Chris shared with me that when Mandela pre-pared to depart after dinner, he shook Mandela's hand and Mandela said, "Chris, you are now shaking the hand of the next president of South Africa." The normally self-effacing Mandela had had a rare moment of predicting the expected outcome. Chris told me this story at a farewell dinner that he and his wife Pam hosted for me when my assignment in Dur-ban ended.

The National Party, which had governed for decades, now had to share legislative and political power with the dominant ANC and other parties proportionally in the first multiparty democracy South Africa had known. Election night was celebratory and joyous for the majority population, as one would expect. I recall sharing the moment with friends, then going home to sleep while reflecting on a day for which so many had worked so hard. We were just glad we got through the historic day. I had dispatched my staff throughout the country so that our reporting covered all of the key areas of Natal and KwaZulu. As always, I had tried hard to maximize and value every staff member's unique talent and abilities.

Many high-profile personalities visited Durban in the run-up to the elections. Celebrities like – Danny Glover, Angela Bassett, and Stevie Wonder came promoting peace while also urging all South Africans to vote. I hosted receptions in my official residence for many of these visitors as well as groups of South Africans. Scores of U.S. citizens from government, think tanks, the artistic world and civil society coming to promote peaceful elections, and to establish new economic partnerships in a rapidly changing South Africa.

Seeking to promote peace and reduce violence, I established the Martin Luther King, Jr., Peace Awards to recognize individuals and groups in KwaZulu-Natal who had made progress in mending fences of strife. Individuals and organizations were nominated by their communities. A committee from our consulate chose the winners. I invited U.S. actor Danny Glover to deliver keynote remarks at one of the award presentation luncheons that I had organized to celebrate the winners. Invitees were thrilled to meet and interact with Glover, many of whom were unaware of his social activism and fight against apartheid.

The charismatic former prime minister of Jamaica, Michael Manley, headed a delegation of European Union (EU) observers to Durban. Jamaica had been the first country worldwide to impose sanctions on apartheid South Africa. Because I as a mid-level officer had met Mr. Manley while covering his political party in Jamaica, I was especially pleased to be able to host the EU delegation—and Mr. Man-ley—at my official residence of the U.S. consul general.

I made frequent visits to the modest home of Mrs. Noku-khanya Bhengu Luthuli in Groutville that she had shared with her beloved late husband Chief Albert Luthuli, ANC President and stalwart. Chief Luthuli, who had been not only a stalwart ANC president but also Africa's first Nobel Peace Prize laureate. Mrs. Luthuli was both a teacher and a grand-daughter of a Zulu chief.

On one occasion, I arranged for a courtesy visit from Mrs. Coretta Scott King to fulfill Mrs. King's wish to meet Mrs. Luthuli. The two widows of Nobel Peace Prize laure-ates met at the home of Ma Bhengu (as I called Mrs. Lu-thuli). Bringing those two great women together for a few precious moments is something I will always cherish.

Photograph taken during the historic meeting of two widows of Nobel Peace Prize winners. Mrs. Coretta Scott King is at left, Mrs. Nokukhanya Bhengu Luthuli in the center, and Pamela Bridgewater is kneeling at right.

Impressions of Mandela

On one occasion, Mr. Mandela was speaking at the University of Natal in Durban. The University of Natal merged with the University of Durban Westville and is now the University of KwaZulu-Natal. Although thousands of us sat in the audience, Mr. Mandela somehow spotted me and beckoned. He always extended a special greeting to me if he knew I was attending an event.

Two of my colleagues in Pretoria—Don Steinberg, later an ambassador to Angola, and Phil Goldberg, later an ambassador to The Philippines—subsequently told me that "Madiba" (Mandela's clan name) would often inquire, if he didn't see me, "Now, where's Pamela?"

On another occasion during my time in South Africa, I was asked to attend an ANC rally in the "colored" township of Atteridgeville, a short distance outside Pretoria. Mandela was a stickler for punctuality. In fact, some would say that he was punctual to a fault. On this occasion, he was, as usual, right on time, but the sound equipment hadn't yet arrived. Sitting in front of the gathered diplomats, he turned around and spotted me. With some unexpected time on his hands, he penned a note, asking, "Who are the people there with you?" I responded, providing the names of the U.S. officers who were with me, and then, almost as a filler, I added the names of the other diplomats in attendance, all of whom, to their delight, he later acknowledged by name.

I would routinely invite first-tour officers to accompany me on occasions such as this, hoping that a few might even get to meet Mandela. That day in Atteridgeville, several got that honor. "Pamela Bridgewater and the Americans," Mandela quipped with a smile, "they always have a very big delegation."

It was on this same occasion that I first met Richard Stengel. Richard later served as a television analyst and as an Undersecretary for Public Affairs and Public Diplomacy at the State Department. At this time, however, he was in South Africa ghostwriting, *Long Walk to Freedom: The Autobiography of Nelson Mandela.*

The ANC rally at which I first met Richard was near November, and I subsequently invited him and others, including two young ANC officers with worked in Mr. Mandela's office, to my home in Pretoria for Thanksgiving dinner. I was moved by Rick's stories about Mr. Mandela's discipline. Rick told us that Mandela would arrive at ANC headquarters at 5:30 in the morning, and record his experiences, speaking into a tape recorder, sharing details that ultimately became the best-selling *Long Walk to Freedom: The Autobiography of Nelson Mandela.*

Umkhonto we Sizwe (MK), translated as "Spear of the Nation," was the armed wing of the ANC and was classified as a terrorist organization by the Department of State. Mandela was classified as a "terrorist" because he was a member of MK, which had engaged in an armed struggle against apartheid structures. Mr. Mandela's name therefore was on the Department of State's terrorist list. This meant that any travel by Mandela to the U.S. had to be approved in advance by the Department of State. It became very cumbersome for the embassy to request a waiver each time Mandela was invited to visit the U.S. to receive an award or attend other important functions. It was years after the transition to a nonracial government and after Mandela's election as president that his name finally was removed from the terrorist list.

For a man larger than life and for one who inspired awe and respect around the world, Mandela was in so many ways a very normal and unassuming individual. He possessed special qualities that were difficult for some to understand. Despite having endured 27 years of imprisonment, Nelson Mandela was a man who did not display rancor. After he was released from prison and became president, Mandela invited the wives of the wardens who had guarded him and the widow of the architect of apartheid to tea. While much was written about these gestures, for Mandela, it was, I believe, simply the civil thing to do.

Mandela was also an individual who displayed normal characteristics and behaviors. One example stands out. When the Governor Lawrence Douglas "Doug" Wilder, visited South Africa, I arranged for him to meet Mandela in his home in Soweto. Governor Wilder was the first black governor of the Commonwealth of Virginia. I was assigned the duty of scheduling activities, accompanying Governor

Wilder, attending his meetings, taking notes, and sending those reports to Washington policymakers. My duties entailed traveling with the governor's delegation on a private Lear jet to all his meetings throughout South Africa. It was quite an amazing time.

Mr. Mandela held his meeting with Wilder over a dinner that Mandela hosted at his Soweto home. When we arrived, Mandela himself opened the door, not a butler or housekeeper but the great man himself. During the dinner, Mandela told his guests that wardens would search his and other prisoners' body cavities for contraband, yet during our meal, Mandela expressed neither rancor nor ill will toward the wardens. One could wish that the positive qualities that Mandela exuded in such large measure—loyalty, punctuality, and self-lessness, along with his lack of rancor—were emulated by other leaders, not just on the African continent but the world over. When elected, he pledged, "I will serve one term," and he did just that.

The Inauguration

I found it exhilarating to see a country reborn. For South Africa, Nelson Mandela's inauguration was not the beginning but the end. Much remained to be done to cement the electoral win and the transition to new governance structures and personalities.

I was stationed in Durban, serving in the newly named province of KawZulu-Natal. But as preparations proceeded for the inauguration of South Africa's new president, Ambassador Lyman called to say he wanted me to assist in Pretoria because the U.S. would be sending a large, high-level delegation to Mr. Mandela's inauguration. Vice President Al Gore would be leading the delegation, which would include First Lady Hillary Rodham Clinton, Tipper Gore, General Colin Powell (Ret.), the Reverend Jesse Jackson, Baltimore Mayor Kurt Schmoke, and many others.

Ambassador Lyman wanted me to serve as First Lady Hillary Clinton's escort officer. I never anticipated that a few years later we would be working together as Secretary of State and U.S. Ambassador.

The atmosphere in Pretoria on inauguration day was joyous. Euphoric might be a better description. I wondered for a while if I had merely dreamed that there had been non-racial elections. Would I wake up to a different reality? But when the head of the South African Defense Force, General Kat Liebenberg, saluted Mandela, I realized that this was no dream: the once imprisoned Nelson Mandela was now commander in chief of the South African Defense Force. Shortly thereafter, fighter jets of the South Africa Defense Force flew over with the colors of the new Rainbow Nation flag spraying from their jets, tipping their wings in salute. President Nelson Mandela had taken the oath of office: he was duly installed!

I had spent many days and nights wondering if, when, and how the transition would take place—and what the outcome would be. Ambassador Swing, Ambassador Lyman, and our entire mission staff were extraordinarily engaged. This multi-level engagement was critically important in effecting what we, our diplomatic colleagues, and South Africans of goodwill were able to accomplish. The United States played a very significant role.

Ambassador Lyman hosted a reception after the inauguration so that members of the official delegation could meet important interlocutors. For embassy staff, official receptions such as this were always working events. Knowing this, Mrs. Clinton, Mrs. Lyman and I had a small bite to eat before the reception even began. "You know all the key personalities in the country," Ambassador Lyman had told me. "So I want you to be sure that Mrs. Clinton is introduced to everyone she should interact with."

One of the key people to whom I was able to introduce First Lady Hillary Clinton on that inauguration day was Helen Suzman, a white South African who had been very active in the anti-apartheid movement. Although she was advanced in age, she remained quite active and had become a close, trusted friend of Mandela, whom she fondly referred to as "Nelson." Because Mrs. Suzman was unable to attend in person, I called her during the reception, informing her that Hillary Clinton wished to speak with her. She was incredulous. I insisted I was not kidding. The two women then spoke, and Mrs. Clinton subsequently invited Mrs. Suzman to the White House.

More Mandela Moments

Mandela often traveled to Durban. Each time he spotted me at a public event, he'd greet me. He was always available to share a few words of greeting with me despite throngs hoping for a chance to touch his hand or take a photograph. I recall one of his many visits to Durban. Sonia Gandhi, the widow of Rajiv Gandhi, had come to Durban to address a large gathering of the Indian community. More people of Indian descent live in South Africa, especially in KwaZulu-Natal, than in anywhere else in the world. During the reception that followed Mrs. Gandhi's address, Mandela motioned to me, saying in his usual kind and thoughtful way, "Come, come, Pamela. I want to introduce you to Sonia." Then, turning to Sonia, he said, "Sonia, this is the U.S. consul general. She is very important." Needless to say, on subsequent occasions, whenever Mandela visited KwaZulu-Natal, I made sure to attend so I could greet him.

As my tour of South Africa drew to an end, I began being invited to numerous large farewell events given in my honor. The diamond magnate, Harry Oppenheimer, and his wife Bridgette hosted a dinner at their Durban home. Vivian Reddy, head of Edison Electric, hosted a farewell party attended by a broad cross section of South Africans. Noted filmmaker Anant Singh and his wife Vanashee, whom he had met at a dinner I had previously hosted for U.S. artist and filmmaker Gordon Parks, invited me to an event. And Successful businessman Don Mkwanazi, not wanting to be outdone, hosted me at yet another fantastic gathering.

However, my most unexpected farewell was hosted by His Majesty King Goodwell Zwelethini, a direct descendant of the famous warrior strategist King Shaka Zulu, who had united many Zulu warriors, leading to a rise in the power of the Zulu nation. King Zwelethini referred to me as "my sister." I often visited the king in Nongoma, his ancestral home, a four-hour drive from Durban. I had attended his fifth marriage (Zulu men are allowed to marry six women legally). I also mentored one of his daughters, Princess Siubusile, as she navigated her path in urban Durban during her school years. Her father, the king never forgot this kindness and always had a very special greeting and welcome for me.

The new mayor of Durban, Obed Mlaba, and the new premier of KwaZulu-Natal, Dr. Frank Mdlalose, also hosted extraordinary gatherings to bid me "Hamba Kahle" (go well!). Their banquets featuring a sumptuous array of foods, showcasing the many palates of KwaZulu-Natal, combined with local beverages and specially created libations, made for epicurean heaven. The dancing, the colorful and pulsating music, and the guests adorned in national dress made these gatherings unforgettable. Sendoffs such as these allowed me to bid special goodbyes to the scores of friends and contacts I had made on my journey building bridges in South Africa's troubled waters.

As tours of duty come to an end, it is customary to pay courtesy farewell calls on major official contacts, particularly those individuals and interlocutors one had engaged in the course of one's work. I had many such appointments to schedule in KwaZulu-Natal and other parts of South Africa. I had met people from all over.

I believed that President Manela would allow me a few minutes in his office to say goodbye. But when Kari Johnson, my assistant, returned after making a call, she reported, "He doesn't just want to say goodbye to you. He wants you to have lunch with him at his residence in Johannesburg!" Later, when she handed me the schedule for my last official day in South Africa, she had written in a blue Sharpie: "Lunch with Madiba," plus a smiley face and the appointed time: 12:30. I kept going over those words, incredulous that I would be afforded such a singular honor. I was not just meeting with a revered ANC leader who had been thankfully now released from exile. Rather, I was having lunch that day with the president of South Africa! No ambassador, no note-taker, no photographer—just the two of us!

I flew up from Durban to Johannesburg, where I would board my international flight to the U.S. President Mandela and I shared a meal and warm conversation at his residence. He asked *my* thoughts about KwaZulu-Natal in the days ahead. I gingerly ventured an assessment, suggesting that while there would certainly be some bumps in the road, I nevertheless hoped—and believed—that the South African people would move ahead to build a peaceful and inclusive nation of opportunity, cherishing respect for everyone. The desperate need for real change for all South Africa's people was paramount in both our minds.

The only interruption came at 1 p.m. when Mandela's housekeeper brought in a portable radio so he could listen to the BBC news! He explained to me that he had formed this habit during his imprisonment. Long-term inmates like himself had been allowed only this one small window to the outside world. When lunch ended, Mandela wished me well with a hug, and I promised to maintain contact. He left our lunch with Tokyo Sekwale, an ANC stalwart, who had come to accompany Mandela to an engagement. Tokyo took a photo of the two of us smiling broadly from the porch of Mandela's residence. That photograph is my favorite of all the many photographs I have with Nelson Mandela.

I had thought that my lunch in Johannesburg would be the last moments I would have with "Madiba." However, we were able to meet again briefly when I returned several years later to participate in a World AIDS conference in Durban, South Africa.

After that memorable lunch in Johannesburg, my assigned driver took me to the international airport. When I first came to South Africa, the airport had been called Jan Smuts International. But by the time of my departure, with so many momentous changes underway all through South Africa, the airport's old name was no more. It was now proudly the Oliver R. Tambo International Airport.

Photograph taken by Tokyo Sekwale, catching smiles on the faces of Nelson Mandela and Pamela Bridgewater, just after their memorable lunch at the president's Johannesburg residence.

I departed Johannesburg for Washington after six unforgettable and impactful years and memories that would last a lifetime. I had received my onward assignment, and the curtain was lowered on my six-year diplomatic mission treading, crossing, bridging, and calming many troubled waters.

Upon his retirement from active political life, Mandela created a foundation for children and continued his work and advocacy for social justice, HIV/AIDS relief, and gender equality. He knew when it was time to move on. I admired him so much for taking on the reigns of leadership at this late period in his life when he could have just enjoyed the perks of having his freedom and basking in the adoring glow that continued to surround him until his death.

Mandela didn't consider himself free until his country-men and women were free too: free to enjoy the liberties of democracy and free to enjoy a "rainbow nation" in which people of all colors are able to live together in peace and prosperity.

Mandela's death at age 95 capped a life of inestimable importance not only to South Africa but to the world. He was the first to say he was not a man without flaws, as we all are. But his qualities of perseverance, patriotism, humanity, loyalty and an uplifting of social justice were lasting and meaningful.

> Pamela Bridgewater established a degree of trust and confidence with Mr. Mandela and the ANC leadership that the United States had not previously enjoyed.
>
> *— Princeton Lyman,*
> *Former U.S. Ambassador to South Africa*

On Mandela's passing, I was asked by the Department of State to share thoughts about this man for the *State Magazine* from my close vantage of him during my assignment in South Africa. I was honored to be asked to write an article that would be published alongside reflections penned by one of the United States' most distinguished diplomats, Ambassador Edward Perkins, the first black U.S. ambassador to South Africa. The joint title was "Two Diplomats Look at Mandela."

Pamela Bridgewater

First Black Woman Consul General

onsul General Pamela Bridgewater (above), the longest serving U.S. diplomat in South Africa, has won plaudits for her work from her superiors, olleagues and from the people of South Africa. The former campus queen greets President Mandela (below) in Chatsworth.

Veteran diplomat brings variety of experiences to Durban post

Text and photography
D. Michael Che

PAMELA Bridgewater is a confident, assertive seasoned diplomat. As consul general of United States Consulate in Durban, this fo campus queen tackles her daily sun-up to down schedule with remarkable calmness. most of the time. To work for the C.G., as she is called must adhere to Bridgewater rule number one: promptne

Hastily walking through the consulate's narrow halls Bridgewater, armed with paperwork and an apple for h glances at her watch and realizes she may be late fe appointment to inspect Siyaphambili club, a U.S.-funded al community garden project located about a two-hour north of the city. She gets ruffled when she spots her new ver, who is still trying to get petty cash for the toll booth

"When I'm ready to go, you need to be ready, too, says in a soft but stern voice. The following day the dri ready when the C.G. tries to squeeze in an afternoon vi Groutville to see Nokukhanya Luthuli, the 92-year-old w of former ANC president and Nobel Laureate Albert Lu This time as the driver pulls away from the curve he b hard to keep from hitting a predestrian. Bridgewater him that look. But, rather than rile him further, she spec a compassionate reassuring tone. Looking through the view mirror at his boss, the driver manages a small sm relief.

Pictured above is an Ebony article about Pamela Bridgewater's assignment as the first African American Consul General in Durban, South Africa, written by photojournalist D. Michael Cheers.

The following anecdotes about my experience in South

Africa were written by two former colleagues, Baxter Hunt

and Ambassador Bernadette Allen, both of whom I mentored

and worked with early in their careers. Submissions like these make me realize the impact I had on others was just as important as the work I did with icons like Nelson Mandela.

Remembering Pamela Bridgewater

I first met Pamela Bridgewater in 1993, when she was Consul General in Durban, South Africa. I had just arrived for my second tour in the Foreign Service, along with my wife and three young children. Durban was a small post, the kind of place where a good or bad boss would make all the difference in your experience. It quickly became obvious to me that I had lucked out – Pamela was the consummate professional and a lovely person. I learned a great deal from her over the next two years, both about how to advance U.S. interests in a complex environment and about how to effectively lead a team.

The U.S. Consulate General in Durban had a diverse staff of local employees. All had been born and raised in the region, but their ancestors were from South Africa, Europe and South Asia. This diversity put us ahead of the curve in a country that was just emerging from apartheid – where different racial groups were forcibly separated - but it also presented challenges in terms of getting everyone to overcome prejudices and stereotypes.

Pamela, as an African American woman, was the perfect choice to represent the United States in Kwa-Zulu-Natal and to lead and unify our team. She was a trailblazer in the U.S. Foreign Service, someone who personified our aspiration, in the words of Martin Luther King, Jr., to be a nation where our children "will not be judged by the color of their skin, but by the content of their character." Her leadership of the Consulate General sent a message to our South African partners of all colors and to all of our locally employed staff.

The content of Pamela's character was extraordinary. She developed personal relationships with all the important players in the region, from Chief Buthelezi to ANC officials, from Afrikaner sugar barons to Indian restaurateurs. She had a gift for connecting with everyone she met, no matter how famous or how humble they were. My wife saw this when she traveled with Pamela to remote villages, where we were using U.S. self-help grants to assist micro-businesses.

One of the many lessons I learned from Pamela, and one that I have tried to replicate throughout my career, is to treat everyone with respect and appreciation for their contributions. Many years later, when I was Charge d'Affaires at the U.S. Embassy in Chile, I made sure to exchange greetings with everyone I encountered at the embassy, including the local guard force and the cafeteria staff.

I greatly appreciated Pamela's attention to mentoring and coaching her team. She took a strong interest in our professional development, and we all benefited from her willingness to delegate meaningful tasks. I was in a consular/management position, but Pamela allowed me to also do reporting work, which aided my development as a political officer. I remember in particular a series of cables she allowed me and our locally employed political assistant to contribute to regarding the root causes of violence in the region. I took this lesson with me throughout my career: give your team more responsibility, be there to coach them as needed, and you will have a more productive, happier group of colleagues–Everyone wins.

The most exciting experience during my two years in Durban came in 1994, when South Africa held its first all-race elections, won by the ANC and Nelson Mandela. The run-up to those elections was a tense time throughout the country, including in KwaZulu-Natal, where competition between the Inkatha Freedom Party and the ANC sometimes led to violence. Pamela recognized that this was a seminal moment for the country, and she made sure that the U.S. Consulate General was visibly supporting the transition from apartheid to democracy. Instead of waiting out the process in our offices high atop the Durban Bay Building, she encouraged us to follow her lead by serving as international monitors for the elections, which many of us did. We went through training on our responsibilities and personal security at the polling places and fanned out across the region on election day.

I will never forget watching South Africans of color waiting patiently in line for hours so that they could, for the first time, select their own national leaders. Thanks to Pamela's leadership, we were part of that great day, part of the eyes and ears that gave confidence to the electorate and that declared the elections had been free and fair.

Pamela was beloved in South Africa. She had served in Pretoria before coming to Durban, and the country's political leaders, including Nelson Mandela, already knew and respected her. It was thanks to Pamela that I got to shake the great man's hand on one of his visits to Durban. But Pamela's attention to family was just as important and just as impactful for me. She always took the time to ask Consulate General staff members how their families were doing, showing that she cared about them personally, not just professionally.

This is something that we Americans often don't make ourselves available for in the workplace, yet it makes a huge difference to our colleagues, especially overseas. Even twenty-five years after we were together in Durban, Pamela still remembers and asks about my wife, my children and my parents. And I still remember Pamela's amazing mother Mary, who was a regular visitor to Durban and who was just as loving and sharp as Pamela, even at an advanced age. The apple does not fall far from the tree.

Remembering Pamela Bridgewater

My assignment as a Deputy Director of Consular Training at the Foreign Service Institute provided me with an opportunity to visit Pamela. By that time, she had advanced to the position of Principal Officer in Durban, South Africa. I had been tasked to conduct a two-week regional training workshop in Côte d'Ivoire for consular officers and locally employed consular staff from U.S. embassies across the African continent, thus I decided to reach out to Pamela Bridgewater about visiting with her for a week in South Africa after I completed the training workshop. She graciously agreed to accommodate me and went the extra mile to ensure a memorable visit.

Until my visit to Durban, I had always considered myself especially adventurous, but I would soon find that my mentor had me beat. Pamela had arranged visits to Victoria Falls and Elephant Isle in Zimbabwe. Upon arrival at Victoria Falls, a guide informed us that the region was experiencing a drought, but I found the mist-producing falls did not disappoint and met my expectations as a wonder of the world. To follow the visit at the falls, Pamela had booked a flight on a two-passenger prop plane to take us to Elephant Isle.

We were given a 10-pound luggage limitation, which required us to leave the remainder of our personal goods in a locker at the airport. I recall asking Pamela whether, in the event something happened to the pilot, she knew how to fly a plane, pointing out that I had no such experience. She confirmed that she did not have pilot skills, but she did not appear concerned. I, on the other hand, had some trepidation and prayed silently the entire time we were in flight, occasionally glimpsing at the scenic view. Fortunately, it was a relatively short flight (a little over an hour) and the skilled pilot, Chris, safely landed the prop plane in a barren space in the savanna. As we awaited pick up to lodging, a herd of elephants strode about ten feet from our position, with no apparent interest in the plane or us, a truly awesome sight and thrill. Shortly thereafter, we heard in the distance a jeep approaching; it was the party that would take us to our lodging for the night.

Upon arrival at the home of the resort owners, I soon learned that Pamela and I were to sleep overnight in one of the guest tents camped a stone's throw away from a lake that was a habitat for hippos. It was too close for comfort for me, as I instantly recalled the danger of hippos from my earlier tour of duty in Bujumbura, Burundi. The resort owner kept assuring us there was nothing to fear, but I could not get over the darkness as it was falling nor the sound of the grunting hippos nearby. I suggested that I would be fine sleeping poolside outside the home of the resort owners that was up the hill. The resort owners insisted that all would be safe, that they had yet to have an incident at the lake. Pamela, clearly sensing my anxiety, intervened and inquired about other possible sleeping arrangements. Eventually, the resort owners relented to our request to abandon the lakeside camp, but insisted we not sleep poolside. Instead, they kindly allowed us to sleep in bedrooms in their home. The whole scene is as vivid in my mind now as it was decades ago, an unforgettable test of negotiation skills.

After our return to Victoria Falls the next day, we went on safari, saw more majestic elephants, graceful gazelles and other animals, visited a local market where I purchased wood and ostrich egg carvings, then closed the visit with a sundowner cruise on the Zambezi River to watch one of the most beautiful sunsets one can imagine. After our return to Durban, I observed Pamela's engagement with staff and host country contacts, as well as her command at official events that she hosted and her presence at events that she attended on behalf of the U.S. Government. I internalized what I had observed, putting what I had learned into practice in my future assignments of greater responsibility. This was my experience with Pamela Bridgewater in South Africa.

—*Ambassador Bernadette Allen (Retired)*

CHAPTER 9

THE ISLANDS OF THE BAHAMAS

Midway into their tours of duty, or sometimes sooner, Foreign Service Officers begin thinking about where they want to serve next: what will be a good onward assignment?

After serving in South Africa for nearly four and a half years, all of which were remarkably busy, I had not thought much about my next assignment. Nor was I especially concerned about landing a career-enhancing next assignment, based on my strong performance two grades higher than my personal grade at the time. The work I was doing in South Africa was well known within the department. I thought I would likely go back to Washington, perhaps as an office director or something similar with increased supervisory responsibilities. I began perusing the list of openings.

One uncommonly quiet late afternoon, near the close of my official workday in Durban, I was sitting at my desk enjoying some down time when the telephone rang, bringing me back to reality. It was an unexpected call from the late Janice Clements, who was a super-capable, talented, and committed continuity counselor in the Bureau of Human Resources at the U.S. Department of State. Janice was always on the lookout for assignments that would enable officers from diverse backgrounds to have an opportunity to demonstrate their considerable talent, exceling and gaining a higher profile.

It was still morning in Washington, but Janice was always an early starter. After exchanging warm greetings, she indicated that the ambassador to The Bahamas, Sidney Williams, was seeking an officer to serve as his Deputy Chief of

Mission (DCM). Janice wanted to gauge my interest in being considered.

I was surprised. DCM positions are highly sought. They are career-enhancing opportunities to manage the day-to-day responsibilities of an embassy, including reporting, staff evaluations, mentoring, and team-building. The DCM assumes the helm of all mission activities and agencies and manages the bi-lateral relationship with the host nation when the Chief of Mission (the ambassador) is absent.

I considered several factors: The Bahamas is English speaking and it is a short distance from the States. Therefore, I could easily travel back home when I needed to attend to my aging mother in Virginia. I thanked Janice and told her that I would be happy to speak with Ambassador Williams about the position.

It was the middle of the night in South Africa. I was already in bed but I made sure to be awake and prepared when the scheduled call came from Ambassador Williams. It was a wonderful interview, despite my not being well rested. He spoke about the qualities he sought in a DCM, and I shared my leadership style, explaining my views on how I would approach the responsibilities of being a DCM. He appeared to be genuinely impressed by the interview.

I soon realized that losing a little sleep the night of that interview was well worth it, as shortly thereafter, he informed me that I was his choice for the position. All appropriate U.S. State Department entities signed off on my selection, including the Bureau of Western Hemisphere Affairs. The office of the Director General and the Deputy Secretary of State are among the entities who must concur with senior assignments. The clearance process requires many steps, but I was ultimately selected, headed again to the waters of the Caribbean.

Much More than Sun, Sand, and Sea

In 1993, at the time of my assignment, Nassau was the fiftieth largest U.S. Foreign Service post. The embassy supported numerous non-Department of State federal agencies, including Drug Enforcement Administration (DEA), U.S. Customs, Immigration and Naturalization Service (INS), Citizenship and Immigration Services (CIS), and the U.S. Foreign Agricultural Service. INS and CIS are now among those agencies that fall under the U.S. Department of Homeland Security.

The mission was also home to members of the U.S. Army, Navy, and Coast Guard; an FBI attaché; and a Marine security guard detachment. The largest component was the Drug Enforcement Administration. We also had a two-person detail from the Foreign Agricultural Service. State Department personnel, along with talented local employees, supported this large interagency presence, as well as those agencies' support staffs and dependents.

More than Drugs and Thugs

I knew from the onset of the assignment that there was a significant law-enforcement element that I, as DCM, would have to manage. I coordinated and chaired the Law Enforcement Working Group. DEA's Special Agent in Charge (SAC), Toni Teresi, was a highly effective professional agent. She and I worked closely and productively in coordinating the work of DEA.

Operation Bahamas Turks and Caicos

The centerpiece of our counternarcotics work was a 24-hour surveillance platform, based at the embassy, called Operation Bahamas, Turks and Caicos (OPBAT), which monitored suspicious and unusual maritime and air traffic using radar and other sophisticated detection methodologies. The U.S. Coast Guard, U.S. Army, DEA, as well as air and marine assets in Nassau and two other islands, Exuma and Inagua, worked in tandem to meet our counternarcotics and crime-fighting mandate.

The U.S. embassy had negotiated an arrangement with the government of The Bahamas and the government of the Turks and Caicos, whereby officers from all three countries were aboard the interdiction assets and had the authority to seize and arrest drug traffickers in their territorial waters. We wanted to waste no time in making arrests in keeping with host nation laws. The U.S. Coast Guard, the U.S. Army and DEA each had helicopter and maritime assets for detection and interdiction. Frequently the seized assets that were used by the drug traffickers were retained by the U.S. or turned over to Bahamian officials for use in ongoing counternarcotics activities.

Toni Teresi knew I wanted to get to work right away. Before I made my first entry into the embassy to meet the ambassador and staff, and before I even had time to settle into my office, Toni said she wanted to take me on a helicopter flight to see some OPBAT positions. Away we went in a DEA "helo," à la James Bond, headed for Inagua Island to view OPBAT operations situated there.

Toni had told me that I would get to observe some of DEA's air-based search mechanisms in coordination with ground-level radar We were nearing Inagua for the landing when the radio onboard sounded an alarm, which I learned later is a warning of suspicious boat activity in the area. I thought immediately that this was *not* a staged activity for my benefit but the real deal. The officer on board indicated that he too had spotted the vessel and had communicated the location to the Coast Guard, which he had dispatched a vessel to intercept. The helicopter pilot informed OPBAT headquarters that he had a "package" on board that needed to be returned to Nassau. I took a deep breath, realizing I was the "package." OPBAT did not want me on board in case of a problem as the "helo" trailed the "narco" boat that day. I thought to myself, "Welcome to Nassau, Madame DCM!"

Bye Bye Balloons

When I arrived in Nassau, counternarcotics assets called aerostats were being used. The aerostats were radar dishes used for 24-hour surveillance aimed toward the most used drug trafficking routes, such as the Old Bahama Channel, a favorite path used by traffickers. The aerostats complemented the work of the OPBAT situation room, which monitored likely criminal activity.

Shortly after my arrival in Nassau, the U.S. decided to dismantle the aerostats and utilize Relocatable Over-the-Horizon Radar. Our Bahamian partners wanted the balloons to remain, as they considered the sheer size and presence of the big dishes a major deterrent to would-be drug smugglers. However, the cost to maintain and repair the huge satellites made them prohibitively expensive, so that fight was lost.

We would often get large seizures of illegal drugs in what seemed like a never-ending battle. Partner officials from The Bahamas, Turks and Caicos communicated and coordinated with me constantly. As the DCM, a significant portion of my daily work was close coordination with DEA, Navy, Army, Coast Guard, FBI, and Narcotics Affairs personnel. I held weekly meetings, seeking to maximize the efforts of the interagency team. I welcomed this new, broad level of responsibility.

I insisted to all of the agency heads that there be "no surprise" operations. I wanted to be kept fully briefed at all times on anything that could impact or jeopardize our bilateral relations. I received many such calls in the middle of the night. The complexities of working through interagency matters and ensuring an appropriate and effective team response proved both instructive and challenging, preparing me for unforeseen things to come.

In addition to narcotics trafficking, I also had to deal with migrants seeking to enter the United States illegally. Most of these were Haitian or Cuban. Several islands of The Bahamas are located in close proximity to Florida, making them a possible gateway for illegal entry into the United States.

On one occasion, our Coast Guard attaché arranged for me to board one of the interdicted migrant boats that had a false bottom for human smuggling. Once on board, I asked to see the inside of the cargo hold. Climbing aboard the creaky, leaky, unsightly vessel—used by desperate migrants who were promised entry into America through The Bahamas—I felt first-hand the desperation that drives individuals to risk life and limb to seek a better way of life. It was sobering, to say the least, and my experience that day will always be difficult to ignore or forget.

Photograph courtesy of Coast Guard Liaison Rick Pineiro

Years later, Coast Guard Liaison Officer Rick Pineiro and I met for lunch in Washington, D.C. We discussed my visit to the migrant boat moored in Nassau Harbor. He told me he had been surprised that I wanted to see the boat. He had thought we would just drive to the dock and view the boat from our vehicle. When I got out of the car, he was somewhat concerned. The boat was anchored at a decrepit dock in an isolated area. When I said I wanted to climb aboard, he quickly explained that migrant boats at sea were almost always in such dangerous shape that Coast Guard crews would often flip a coin to decide who would risk going aboard to do the final sweep after the migrants had been transferred to a Coast Guard cutter. The sweep team would often then burn the boats at sea, knowing that they couldn't be safely towed. So when I said that I wanted to look inside the main hold of the boat, his first thought was, "Well, if the Deputy Chief of Mission is injured, at least it will be a quick trip back to district headquarters in Miami to explain what happened."

I never knew, of course, that I had caused the Coast Guard Liaison Officer such concern. Thankfully, it all worked out. To this day, however, images and thoughts from my boarding that boat are as strong as if it happened yesterday.

Unexpected Adventure at Sea

On an official visit to Spanish Wells, one of the many inhabited islands of The Bahamas known for its succulent lobster and other seafood delicacies, I encountered troubled waters of an unexpected nature.

Charles Fernander, the embassy's senior security assistant and a respected retired member of the Royal Bahamian Police Force, organized the visit and accompanied me on what I thought of as an orientation trip to Spanish Wells. His wife Sylvia accompanied us.

The day was picture perfect, with blue skies, calm wind, and the glistening of the crystal-clear, blue water of the Atlantic Ocean. Mr. Fernander and the mayor of Spanish Wells wanted to take me out on the water to see the vast opportunities for illegal activity and thus the need for more resources to intercept and deter criminal activity. We donned our life vests and climbed aboard the small boat with our host, the mayor of Spanish Wells, who planned to describe the problems the island faced, making a pitch for additional U.S. assistance for assets and personnel.

The boat took off, but the engine stalled within a few feet. After drifting back to shore, the captain assessed the problem, made a few tweaks, and we were once again on board. Yet again, the engine sputtered, then shut off, and we returned. That should have been my cue to say, "Let us do this another time," but being the bridge builder that I was and not wanting to offend our host, I figured that the third time would be the charm.

It appeared that the boat was indeed sailing smoothly this time, but sometime after we had made our way into deeper blue water, the engine stopped again. We were three individuals and a captain (all older than me), plus Mrs. Fernander, who had recently had heart surgery. The only "equipment" we had to work with were stick paddles and no form of communication, cell service not being available at sea. The three of us, with the exception of Mrs. Fernander, began paddling. Fortunately, the waters were calm, and with some steady paddling and a few prayers, we managed to get close enough to shore to beckon to some persons we saw there, asking them to help pull us ashore, where we were able to make a phone call. Our rescuers were Haitians. We phoned the mayor's office and informed his son of our plight.

We were told that a tow boat would be dispatched to bring us back to port in Spanish Wells. So we climbed back aboard the boat and continued to paddle with all our might along the shoreline until finally we saw a speeding tow boat coming to tow us back to port. We were very grateful to the Haitians who had assisted us.

A Star Arrives

Late one evening, during December 1997, after I had turned in for the night, I received a phone call from the Department of State and our local Coast Guard. They told me that the Coast Guard had interdicted an illegal vessel in Bahamian waters. This wasn't the usual boat filled with desperate people seeking escape from political persecution or economic deprivation. Onboard was one of Cuba's star baseball pitchers, Orlando "El Duque" Hernandez.

I gathered myself and hurriedly went to the building where Hernandez and two other people were being detained for interrogation by U.S. Customs, Bahamian Customs and the U.S. Coast Guard. Hernandez was a former member of the Cuban national baseball team. The Cuban government had banned him from playing baseball for life, suspecting that during competition at non-Cuban locations, he might try to follow his brother Livan, also a pitcher, who had begun playing baseball in the U.S. El Duque indicated he had made the boat trip hoping to get an opportunity to play baseball in the U.S. Although the Cuban government did not look favorably upon such behavior, the Department of State authorized me to offer him asylum.

Hernandez was traveling with a female companion and another man. He said the asylum offer needed to be extended to all three people. When it wasn't, Hernandez chose to remain in The Bahamas. Baseball agent Joe Cubas subsequently arrived and arranged for Hernandez and his party to go to the Dominican Republic. Hernandez departed The Bahamas after much publicity and all the excitement that his presence on the small island had generated. He seemed to relish it, as did the Bahamian residents who got to interact with the affable athlete on the streets of Nassau.

Hernandez's saga made national news and a 60 minutes news team was on hand for his departure from The Bahamas.

After El Duque's subsequent arrival in the Dominican Republic, he was offered a lucrative contract with the New York Yankees. He played for multiple major league teams prior to his retirement.

Strong Bilateral Partner

The government of The Bahamas has traditionally been a strong bilateral partner with the U.S. on many issues of importance, including human rights and the guaranteeing of civil liberties, as well as support for the U.S. on many issues that come before the United Nations. Even amid differences of opinion, the relationship remained friendly. As a result, throughout my tenure in The Bahamas, we were able to iron out, whenever necessary, a mutually respectful compromise.

Cultural Diplomacy/Opera Comes to Nassau

The U.S. has long recognized the importance of sharing our cultural platform through art, music and education. A highlight for me was arranging for Simon Estes, an internationally renowned bass/baritone opera star, to visit Nassau for a series of concerts. The concerts helped to raise money to support women's and children's programs in The Bahamas, with a focus on improved health outcomes. The performances were a huge hit with the Bahamian people. Ambassador Arthur Schechter was now chief of mission.

The Bahamas Governor General served as patron for one of the performances, which was held at Christ Church Cathedral, a beautiful edifice that Simon thought enabled the maximum resonant sound quality. I was pleased that Texaco Bahamas Ltd. under-wrote the full cost of the performance as part of its corporate outreach and community support.

I had first met Simon in South Africa during my tenure there and maintained contact. Simon's deep, beautiful and smooth voice was a showstopper, even before he sang a note. A simple hello would generate a warm feeling in all whom he met. Once we contacted him, he generously agreed to come to The Bahamas for a nominal fee, and Sandals Royal

Bahamian provided its signature all-inclusive lodging. It was a grand occasion for the Bahamian people and for Simon, pianist Don Ryan, and the two European opera singers who accompanied Simon on this trip.

Photograph of the program flyer that Simon Estes autographed for Pamela Bridgewater at the time of his 1999 concert sponsored by Texaco Bahamas Ltd. at Christ Church Cathedral in The Bahamas.

Supporting local charities and vulnerable communities became one of the most important elements of my diplomatic work. Throughout my career, I used my platform as a senior diplomat to bring attention to health issues and other causes that impacted local citizens, especially women and children.

I felt it was important to share as many cultural partnerships as possible with the local community. Whenever possible, I arranged for official visits by cultural icons from the U.S.—especially from my hometown—to promote partnerships that would strengthen and improve people-to-people relations.

One of these visitors was Johnny P. Johnson, a celebrated artist and educator who had been a Virginia Teacher of the Year as well as my own sixth-grade art teacher. He met with local artists, exchanged ideas and techniques, and met with fledgling artists, providing inspiration and examples with his winning personality and talent.

The Bahamian people have a great love of art and music, and the visits by Simon Estes and Johnny Johnson further demonstrated that the U.S.—Bahamian relationship went far beyond our strong partnership in countering illegal drug trafficking and interdicting illegal migrant boats enroute to the United States.

Involving all elements of the U.S. mission in representational activities is one of the ways to generate positive morale among an embassy's staff. Commemorating the Independence of the United States of America is always the most important event on an embassy's calendar, followed by the U.S. Marine Corps birthday ball. For one Fourth of July, the U.S. mission was granted permission to have a parade of staff vehicles on a famous, albeit short, strip along Cable Beach in downtown Nassau. I invited some young children of embassy family members to ride in my white convertible after helping me decorate the car in red, white and blue. They were excited not only to display their artistic talent but also take part in such a significant event.

My Bahamian tour was not without a sad chapter, though, as we lost the wives of two Army pilots who were flying with their husbands in Blackhawk helicopters while their husbands were off duty. This traumatic event shook our entire community. I received he initial call about the incident, after which we in the embassy had to take immediate action, quickly returning the bodies to the U.S. lest any bureaucratic red tape prolong the trauma for the families. Not surprisingly, the pilots themselves also lost their careers as a result of this unofficial and inappropriate use of government property, resulting in the death of their wives.

While this misuse of official assets ended in tragedy, the Blackhawks had an enviable record of not just interdicting illegal narcotic and other criminal activity. During my stay in Nassau, they also performed a lifesaving rescue of a Bahamian mother whose pregnancy was in jeopardy. The mother required an emergency airlift to a hospital from the remote island where she lived. Quick action on the request from the government of The Bahamas and our moving it rapidly up the chain for Army HQ approval resulted in the safe birth of the young Bahamian baby. The call to get approval for that Blackhawk mission was one I was happy to sanction.

When my three-year tour in Nassau came to an end, I learned from my career development counselor that I would be returning to Washington for senior professional training.

CHAPTER 10

BACK TO WASHINGTON / THE 42nd SENIOR SEMINAR

I was selected to participate in the Department of State's prestigious Senior Seminar, an exciting year-long interagency professional training program aimed at those senior foreign affairs and national security officers deemed to have future leadership potential.

I embarked on the department's 42nd Senior Seminar in August 1999, shortly after completing my tour of duty as Deputy Chief of Mission in Nassau. As it happened, shortly after the seminar began, the individual we had elected as our class president resigned from the Foreign Service and thus dropped out of the seminar. I was elected to serve in his place.

Our class of thirty-five included representatives from the U.S. Department of State, the U.S. Agency for International Development, the Central Intelligence Agency, the Foreign Agriculture Service, and each of the branches of the U.S. armed forces. Five of us were African Americans.

My role as president, was to communicate my classmates' interests and concerns to the Senior Seminar Dean and/or Associate Dean and to communicate their views to the class. Mutual communication was important because of the seminar's educational methods, which included experiential teaching, transformative learning where one applies critical thinking, and instrumental learning. Class committees planned the content of regional trips around the U.S., making sure each trip addressed themes chosen by the class members and administrators. The seminar also required each participant to produce a research paper.

Our class was extremely fortunate to have the

distinguished Ambassador Aurelia Brazeal as our dean. She had served as U.S. ambassador in Kenya, Ethiopia, and the Federated States of Micronesia, as well as in other high-level senior assignments. She was the first dean of the Department of State's Leadership and Management School, having played a major role in its creation. She was one of the few African American women in senior leadership positions at the time. (Another was the late Ambassador Ruth A. Davis).

The associate dean of the Senior Seminar was the very able Barry Wells, a Senior Executive Service officer who was later named ambassador to The Gambia. Ambassador Brazeal's example of bold, dynamic leadership and mentoring provided an excellent model that I continued to draw upon throughout my career.

The seminar was organized around thematic modules. Class committee groups were responsible for coordinating the core substantive areas. Speakers were invited, regional trips were planned, and class discussions ensued. Among the themes for discussion were leadership and management, national security, the national economy, the environment, Congress and the U.S. Constitution, crime and the criminal justice system, and the overall state of the nation. We understood that issues within each of these realms could impact the work we would commonly undertake overseas. Ambassador Brazeal expanded our training to include two overarching themes—spirituality in America and race in America—each of which would impact our main subject areas.

During the course of the seminar, we traveled to all the geographic areas of America: the Northwest, Northeast, South, Southwest, and Middle America. Each trip reflected our class research, involved inviting appropriate speakers, reflecting on pre-arranged themes, followed by informal discussions of what we had learned.

On our Northeast trip we visited the "Big Dig" in Boston as it was being constructed. It was an opportunity to learn about the planning for large projects, the mechanics of implementing them, and, most revealing, the politics behind them. A roundtable with a noted *Boston Globe* journalist gave us the chance to interview a national journalist on questions of importance facing our country. Moving on to Gettysburg, Pennsylvania, we relived the tragic Civil War battles that had so moved President Lincoln when he penned his famous Gettysburg Address. Then it was on to Wall Street, where we were briefed on stock market operations by senior officials. A truly thrilling experience was ringing the bell to signal the opening of the New York Stock Exchange, then watching the frenzied action on the floor.

Our trip South to Mississippi and Louisiana enabled us to experience and study the plight of Black Americans in the Mississippi Delta area. Their stories conveyed vivid details of the difficult lives they had lived. We examined public policies and their relevancy to U.S. foreign affairs. When we visited the Vicksburg Civil War battleground, we listened to elderly African American blues master-guitarist "Mr.

Johnny," captivated by stories of his musical journey, swaying and patting our feet to his soulful guitar playing. One of our classmates was bold enough to play along with Mr. Johnny, who warmly welcomed this novice to the stage.

Then it was time to head to the Midwest heartland. I stayed with a family on a working soybean farm, joining the farmer in his daily work and hearing firsthand the challenges of family farmers. During my stay, I vividly recall having to wrap myself in layers of blankets: the indoor heating was scant, and winter was upon us. I also remember climbing aboard a combine with the farm owner, reaping soybeans, which I learned were a major export crop. I also discovered how much technology was involved in farming—for instance, how farmers could access soybean market prices worldwide via computers, and then decide when and where their crops might go.

On the class trip to the Northwest, we toured the Boeing plant in Seattle, where we saw 777 aircraft being assembled.

For those of us who had flown so often, it was a revelation to see the inside of a plane as it was prepared for passenger service.

Each of the military members of the class arranged a trip particular to his branch of service. For example, the Air Force representative organized a trip to the Aviano Air Base in Italy, where we experienced interactions of aircraft maintenance procedures and how those melded with operational requirements. On the flight back, we witnessed a mid-air refueling, which was truly exhilarating: two huge aircraft flying at top speeds, docking perfectly to execute a refueling. Each of us was allowed a few minutes to watch in awe of this process in real time. Not to be outdone, the class's Navy captain arranged a trip to Hawaii. We lodged and experienced life at the Schofield Barracks, then toured the USS *Arizona* memorial, reliving the trauma of the Pearl Harbor attack. My most memorable moment was boarding the nuclear submarine, USS *Columbia*. We not only learned about the inner workings and life aboard a nuclear sub, but we also did a deep dive in the Pacific Ocean. (I called out to the Lord a few times on that exhilarating journey!)

The U.S. Army cohort organized a trip to Fort Bragg, North Carolina, headquarters for special forces training. Again, it was not just theory but practice. Each of us donned heavy military gear as used in training and climbed a ladder, high above the ground, to experience a zip-line whirl to the end of the course. We learned how U.S. Special Forces prepare for combat missions and other military duties.

Adding to the reality of our experiences, we traveled for most of the year by military aircraft. Even for long flights to Europe and elsewhere, we sat straight up and buckled down along the exterior walls of troop-carrying C-130s or on other military aircraft.

Our visit to Bosnia was memorable for several reasons. Between 1992 and 1995, after the disintegration of Yugoslavia, an inhumane plan had been executed to ethnically cleanse Bosnia through systematic killings of non-Serbians, the majority of whom were Bosnian-Muslims. Due to ongoing residual instability, the military escort aboard our plane was armed and on the lookout for anything that might impede our safe landing. It didn't end on landing; we had to navigate through some terrain where we were advised there were still live landmines that had not yet been removed! Thanks for the warning I thought. We never forgot that experience.

In San Diego, we observed portions of a 54-hour Marine training challenge called "the Crucible." Seeing new recruits arrive to stand on the yellow bricks—and then seeing trained recruits marching the "tough last miles over the hill" to finish the Crucible—was truly sobering. Even the toughest men in our class shed a tear at seeing those young recruits singing the Marine Corps hymn as they mastered the final hurdle with the last ounce of their physical strength.

Before we departed San Diego, we were invited to go

aboard the *Bonhomme Richard*, an amphibious personnel carrier, to learn about the life and responsibilities of those assigned to such a vessel. We diplomats wanted to be exposed firsthand to some of the training and preparation that our military counterparts go through. Our job is to find diplomatic solutions to seemingly intractable problems, not only to keep our nation out of wars and to protect American citizens and interests but also to keep our military out of harm's way.

We members of the Senior Seminar boarded the *Bonhomme Richard* and went out to sea, our backpacks full of heavy gear. I was in good shape at that time, but, mind you, I was not a big person.

To my surprise, while on board the *Bonhomme Richard*, my mobile phone rang. It was Ambassador Marc Grossman, the State Department's Under Secretary for Political Affairs. I knew Marc from having served with him some years earlier in Brussels. He told me that I was being considered for an ambassadorship to the Republic of Benin—and asked if I would be interested. The water and waves were splashing vociferously. I thought for a moment that perhaps I had misunderstood, but I then quickly explained where I was and asked if I could respond after I had returned to "dry land."

As I contemplated being considered for this nomination—a potentially lifechanging decision—I phoned the only person I knew with firsthand knowledge of Benin, Ambassador Ruth A. Davis, who had served as ambassador there. She was very positive about Benin and thought I would have a great experience there should l be nominated and selected. I spoke French, so I did not have a language issue, and Benin, though poor and small, was making strides to entrench democratic governance and to improve its economy. Similarly, I had had six years of experience in South Africa as that nation sought to build a more inclusive economy for its previously disenfranchised citizens. So I would be somewhat prepared for what was happening in Benin.

Realizing this was a wonderful opportunity, I agreed to have my name submitted.

My year spent as a member of the 42nd Senior Seminar was truly a chance to retool, re-energize and reconnect with the country and people we represent around the world. It also prepared me to better understand the intersection between domestic and policy. Not only did I leave the seminar better able to understand the cultures of other U.S. national security agencies, but I also found myself more focused on complex problem solving, executive leadership, integrity, the foundations of our democratic society and creating and sustaining coalitions necessary for attaining U.S. diplomatic objectives globally.

The Senior Seminar was abolished in 2001. I regret that this transforming experience is no longer available as it was to my peers and myself. It is needed even more today as our leaders are faced with understanding, serving and representing a more diverse and divided nation.

On another sorrowful note, the *Bonhomme Richard*, on which I got that surprising phone call, was destroyed by fire on July 12, 2020, apparently an act of arson by a disaffected marine. Ironically, I was in San Diego at the time on a consulting assignment with the U.S. Department of Defense. The fire burned for several days, and as I rode past the burning ship, I recalled happier times and recalled as well, of course, that dramatic phone call that I had received from Under Secretary Grossman.

The Process, the Papers—A Long and Winding Road

Not long after I accepted Under Secretary Grossman's offer to be considered for an ambassadorship, I received word that I had indeed been selected as the Department of State's candidate for Ambassador Benin. Shortly thereafter, the vetting process began.

Mounds and mounds of paperwork need to be completed, both for the White House and for other government agencies, including security, medical, financial documents, current and past federal and state income tax records, and a FBI background investigation. The legislative branch at the State Department coordinated the equally large number of forms to be completed and sent to the White House for a final scrubbing and review prior to being submitted to the U.S. Senate, which must confirm all presidential appointees.

In due course, the White House announced that President Clinton *intended* to nominate me as ambassador to Benin. Yes, the White House first announces the president's *intention* to nominate. Only later, following additional scrutiny, did the White House announce that "the president of the United States *today* nominated Pamela E. Bridgewater of Virginia to be the next U.S. Ambassador to Benin."

No words can explain what I felt when the official announcement finally appeared. The words were there for all to read: family, friends, co-workers, former students, neighbors, teachers, and more. Although the reality was still hard for me to fathom, it was now indisputably true: I had been nominated to serve as a U.S. ambassador to Benin!

The next critical step was for me to appear before the Senate Foreign Relations Committee for the confirmation hearing. The officer in charge of the State Department's Benin Desk scheduled appointments for me with key agencies and bureaus serving in Benin. They included USAID, Peace Corps, Diplomatic Security, Consular Affairs and Public Affairs. I met with the State Department's African Affairs Executive Officer, learning about financial resources, budgets, housing and other issues impacting the work in Benin. I also met with representatives of the CIA, the National Security Agency, and others for intelligence briefings. And on and on it went.

Then I had to face the "murder board." Why such an intimidating and foreboding name? The State Department wants would-be ambassadors to be as well-prepared as possible for any questions they might be asked by the senators who sit on the sub-committee for the nominee's assigned region. For me, it was the subcommittee on Africa. So members of the State Department "murder" you with every possible question of relevance or interest to committee members. The State Department's Bureau of Legislative Affairs also arranged for me to pay courtesy calls on committee members, and their staffs, including both legislative and regional personnel. It felt like an endless round of meetings, calls, and briefings, but the preparation I received was an immense gift, provided to me by Joycelyn Mack Brown, the Benin Desk officer, and others who assisted her.

The day for my hearing finally arrived. I made my way to Dirksen Senate Office Building Room 419—I will never forget that room number!—and the hearing began. Two other nominees for African assignments were also to be questioned.

I delivered my opening statement to the members, introduced family members and friends present, including my mother, and thanked the president for the confidence to nominate me. I then expressed what I hoped to achieve "if confirmed." (Lesson one had been never to presume or speak as if one's confirmation was a fait accompli or a "done deal.")

Most of my questions were straightforward, and I was comfortable throughout the process. The only slight curve ball came when a senator asked a sensitive question about Libya. I knew the answer, but due to the classified nature of the response, I indicated I would respond to the committee in writing.

The infamous Sen. Jesse Helms chaired the Senate Foreign Relations Committee from 1995 to 2001, and on the desk where I sat, the notepads available for our use included his name in bold type. His reputation for playing hardball and for putting holds on committee votes created a brief moment of foreboding for me, but I stayed calm and focused. At the conclusion of the hearing, the subcommittee chair thanked family and friends for attending, thanked us nominees for our willingness to serve, and the hearing adjourned.

The Interminable Wait

The next step for nominees is to be voted out of the committee with approval so that the nomination can go before the full Senate for a vote. Senator Helms, however, showed his power and put a hold on all nominees who were awaiting a confirmation vote. We learned that he had a longtime grouse with the Department of State over a World War II debt issue. We waited, and waited, and waited.

It was five months to be exact before Senator Helms released his hold and allowed the nominations to proceed with a full Senate vote. When the vote finally occurred, we were all confirmed in a matter of minutes. The power of committee chairs is truly daunting. Some nominees waited a year or more; some were never confirmed.

The Swearing-In Ceremony

The last and perhaps most exciting step in the confirmation process is the swearing-in ceremony. Until you are sworn in you are referred to as ambassador-designate, and only after the swearing-in are you allowed to be called ambassador.

To be sworn in and take the official oath of office as a United States ambassador is, without a doubt, a singularly unforgettable moment. It was certainly not a bridge I thought I'd ever cross. I took the oath of office and was sworn in at the Department of State's Benjamin Franklin Room. Ambassador Aurelia Brazeal, my dean from the Senior Seminar, administered the oath and delivered remarks.

The Benjamin Franklin Room, named for the first U.S. Secretary of State, is the largest and most stately of all the diplomatic reception rooms in the State Department. It is often used not only by the Secretary of State also by U.S. presidents, vice presidents, members of Congress and other diplomatic organizations. Securing a date on the calendar to hold an event in the Ben Franklin Room is a challenge, particularly if you are hoping to be sworn in over the summer, as each August the room closes for a complete cleaning and facelift.

The process for a swearing-in begins with generating a list of invitees. The list initially comes from the ambassador designate, coordinated with the desk officers for the country where one is to serve. So I began to create my list: family, friends, co-workers, teachers, members of Congress and other government officials with whom I had worked or established personal and professional relations.

In the end, nearly five hundred individuals attended my swearing-in to Benin—many from my hometown. They included my mother Mary (only one week after undergoing triple bypass surgery); first-grade teacher Janie Pratt; aunt Lois Miller; cousins Jackie Miller, Staci, Jared and Dion Pullam, Herb Proctor, and Alex Picou; the mayor of

Fredericksburg and my pastor, the Rev. Lawrence Davies, and his wife Janice Pryde Davies; and a host of others. A dear family friend, Xavier Richardson coordinated two busloads of guests from Fredericksburg. My best friend from college, Christine Johnson and her daughters Alicia and Christie, were present as were former students Max Hilaire, Yvette Taylor and Josie Bass, from my days of teaching at Morgan State and Bowie State.

After that celebratory event, another friend, Darryl F. Marshall, who also served as my financial advisor, invited the *entire* Fredericksburg contingent and other guests to his beautiful home in Fort Washington, Maryland, for a lavish reception. It was a sumptuous feast that included fried turkey (which I had never eaten before), lots of side dishes, beverages of all kinds, two bands, and more fun that any of us could have dreamed of. I felt a bit nervous about two buses driving into the beautiful, quiet, tree-lined Fort Washington neighborhood, but Darryl assured me all would be fine.

The deep pride at my achievement, felt by all those in attendance, was incredibly special to me. As the two Fredericksburg buses headed back down Interstate 95, all on board seemed both joyous and well-satisfied, having even been given a goodie bag for the road. They were headed home—and I would soon be on my way to West Africa as the representative of the president of the United States to the government and people of the Republic of Benin.

Photograph of Pamela Bridgewater with President Bill Clinton, who nominated her to be the U.S. ambassador to the Republic of Benin.

CHAPTER 11

BEGIN THE BENIN

I was a U.S. government civil service employee on a two-year excursion in Cotonou, Benin. I looked forward to completing this temporary overseas assignment and returning to Washington for my civil service employment with the State Department. I did not know that my life and career were changing for the better because of Ambassador Pamela E. Bridgewater.

—Don Curtis,
Retired Foreign Service Officer

When I arrived in the Republic of Benin, located on the coast of West Africa's Atlantic Ocean, I wasn't prepared for the hot, humid climate nearly year-round. Although I had experienced the dog days of summer in

Washington D.C. and its suburbs all my life, the heat in Benin sometimes seemed oppressive. Nevertheless, while the climate required some adjusting, I found it refreshing to encounter people who were naturally kind, welcoming, genuinely warm and easy to meet.

My diplomatic work got off to an incredibly quick start. The first order of the day was to meet with key embassy staff, both local and U.S. The local Benin staff comprised the largest cohort of embassy personnel. I could not have felt more welcome. I spoke to them about my goals as their ambassador and as the U.S. president's personal representative. I considered my work as a leader of a team.

Although there is now a new state-of-the-art embassy compound in Cotonou, Benin, back at the time of my posting, we were a lock-and-leave post meaning we had no Marine security guards to secure the building. Senior officers had keys. We simply locked and unlocked the building as needed.

The U.S. staff consisted of a Deputy Chief of Mission, a political/economic officer, a management officer, a general services officer, a regional security officer, a peace corps director, a USAID director, and a military attaché who was based in Ghana and visited periodically.

Presenting my unofficial credentials to Benin's Foreign Minister was among my first duties. Without the acceptance of credentials, an ambassador is not considered fully on the job. The Foreign Minister was Kolawole Idjj, an internationally recognized and accomplished diplomat who received my preliminary letters of credence, a necessary prelude to my presenting the official copies to the head of state President Mathieu Kérékou. Both of these presentation ceremonies were exciting for me as they signified that I was now officially the U.S. Ambassador to Benin—and thus ready to get to work.

Photograph of Pamela E. Bridgewater meeting with Benin President Mathieu Kérékou after presenting her official credentials as the U.S. ambassador.

Because Benin was one of the poorest countries in West Africa, my mandate as ambassador centered around helping to improve Benin's economic indicators, quality of life, health, education while solidifying Benin's nascent democracy.

President Kérékou had started out as a Marxist leader. He had come to power in a military coup. He had then led the country for 19 years before being stripped of his powers in 1990 when the Benin National Conference sought to move the country toward multiparty democracy. Nicephore Soglo, a lawyer and former Minister of Finance, had won the first multiparty election and became president in 1991. Mathieu Kérékou had returned as president in 1996, this time as a result of a democratic election. Kérékou would later become the first head of state to apologize for those African leaders who had participated in the transatlantic slave trade. A marker near the former slave markets in Richmond, Virginia, acknowledges President Kérékou's historic apology.

I witnessed many memorable and significant things in Benin. The embassy supported a plethora of special self-help projects in the predominantly Muslim in the North of Benin. These were managed by Haoua Riley, an exceptional coordinator who was a master at vetting prospective prospects, visiting the areas and seeing firsthand their needs and capacity to utilize funds that could bring change and improvement to the lives of villagers.

I witnessed an unforgettable project launch during a visit to the north of Benin. The embassy had granted some money to women there in hopes of ending female genital mutilation. Practitioners typically performed these mutilations, painful and traumatic for both young girls and women, for as little as the equivalent to a single U.S. dollar. Yet for many practitioners, that dollar was an important part of their economic livelihood. Thus, the self-help project proposed providing training in alternative skills to give the women new ways of earning money. They could not do so, however, without the consent of the local Imam (Muslim spiritual leader).

My job along with Haoua was to travel north to meet with the chief Imam and other spiritual leaders to show respect to them and, more importantly, to seek their concurrence for the women to cease this practice of genital mutilation and to engage in the self-help project funded by the Ambassador's Special Self-Help fund, the money for which had come from USAID. I succeeded! And for me, that felt like a major achievement.

Haoua was very effective in her work and was affectionately called "Reine du Nord"—Queen of the North—by President Kérékou as word of the U.S. Ambassador's self-help programs spread quickly and widely. Visiting the projects meant trips over rough roads with few breaks for "conveniences," though stopping to eat an Igname "pile," prepared ahead of time by a roadside "chef" who knew my favorite yam dish, always sweetened the journey.

The "Slave" Ship *MV Eterino*

In 2001 there was international attention and concern following reports that a Nigerian registry ship, the MV *Eterino*, had departed the port of Cotonou with trafficked minor children on board. The ship had a record of transporting human cargo for money. It was reported missing after it was denied landing permission in Gabon and Cameroon. Press and journalists from all over, including major U.S.

news outlets, the Department of State, and other agencies were focused on this situation, calling me regularly to check on developments. To monitor the situation, I worked closely with Esther Galuma, who managed, the U.N. Children's portfolio in Benin. At her request, the U.S. provided maritime and other assets to assist in locating the ship.

When the ship was finally located and enroute back to Cotonou with what everyone hoped would be the "missing children," something approaching pandemonium broke out at the port of Cotonou. I was among a throng of reporters, photographers, and cell-phone callers awaiting the ship's arrival.

I had permission, along with other stakeholders, to go aboard the vessel and assess the condition of the minors. After calling Washington in real time, describing the situation, I felt like I could add "reporting live" to my diplomatic capabilities.

Fortunately, the children did not appear to be in distress or maltreated. Family members were also present on the dock to receive the children whom they had "sold" to the ship crew for minimal amounts of money, thinking that the children would receive work in other countries to share with impoverished families back home.

I offered the full support of the U.S. in assisting the children and their families, hoping to prevent future "sales" of their young to work on cocoa farms, as domestics, or in other "employment." I knew well that the transporting of child labor for gain would not stop with these "rescued" children, but also knew that our efforts to help alleviate poverty and provide education and job opportunities must continue as a top U.S. policy priority.

Many local—and highly talented—Beninese staff worked for our embassy. Their work was invaluable. Two of those exceptional people were Firmine Houemavo, the protocol assistant and Sylvie Faboumy, the political assistant. I cannot overstate their outstanding and sustained contributions to our work during my tenure and that of other chiefs of mission. Firmine continued to work for the embassy for 36 years and was promoted regularly. She ended her tenure as the embassy's liaison with Benin's military, facilitating the military's effort to enhance training and professional development.

A true highlight of my experience in Benin was to meet Father Godfrey Nzamujo and learn about the work of the Songhai Center, which he founded and served as director. The Songhai director was both a visionary and Renaissance man. With two doctor of philosophy degrees, Father Nzamujo's work at Songhai was transformative, economically empowering and, frankly, amazing. The late Harry F. Lightfoot, who served as USAID director in Benin, had initially briefed me on the project, which he raved about, calling it one of the best investments of U.S. funding that USAID had ever provided. On the first of my many visits to

Songhai, I was overwhelmed with the vibrancy of what was growing in this organic farming center and with how the concept of "no waste" was being implemented. Utilizing *everything* for repurposing was the order of the day. The dynamic Father Nzamujo seemed to be everywhere doing everything all at once. He was overseeing amazingly healthy crops, teaching women farming techniques, and showing them how to plant gardens to be self-sufficient, as well as farming tilapia and catfish larger than I could have ever imagined. Cashews, corn, soap, chicken and pigs were featured at Songhai, along with other delicacies of Benin, such as agouti (muskrat), which I *never* acquired a taste for. Agouti or not, the Center's Songhai restaurant was *the* place to dine. People regularly made the trek from Cotonou, the commercial capital, to Porto Novo, Benin's official capital (where Songhai was located), for an always fresh, organic and delectable meal.

Father Nzamujo, recognizing the need for technology advances that would benefit the population of Benin, sought the infrastructure that would allow widespread computer hookups and internet usage. I was very pleased to facilitate that technology through a U.S. company, Titan Technologies. Ultimately, a state-of-the-art internet center was erected, named Bridgewater Technology in my honor, something I treasure greatly.

AMBASSADOR BRIDGEWATER TECHNOLOGY CENTER BUILDING

The internet access and speeds at Songhai were the fastest and best in Benin at that time, and perhaps still are, thanks

to Father Nzamujo's ingenuity and the U.S. partnership that
I am proud to have been a part of.

Photograph of office assistant Blandine Araba at Bridgewater Technology Center.

INTERNET MEETING ROOM

Photograph of Father Nzamujo and others at the Bridgewater Technology Center.

When the technology center was dedicated, my late mother Mary made a special visit for the event and was able to witness the dedication ceremony.

AMBASSADOR BRIDGEWATER HEALTH CENTER BUILDING

Exterior photograph of the Ambassador Bridgewater Health Center Building in Benin.

Songhai has grown from strength to strength. It is now a thriving, vibrant conference center and hotel site along with a biotech center for research and development. It boasts a health center for staff and community use, has partnerships and internships with American universities, and exports products to France, including the best natural yoghurt I've ever tasted.

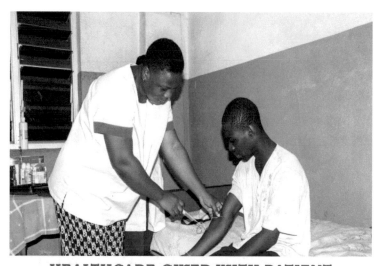

HEALTHCARE GIVER WITH PATIENT

Healthcare professionals provide medical care at the Bridgewater
Health Center.

I have returned to visit Songhai over the years. I continue to marvel at the center's phenomenal accomplishments. Father Nzamujo often tells the story of Songhai being started on a parcel of waste land given to him by the government of Benin, which believed in his vision for development. He founded Songhai with his share of a family inheritance. It has now opened sites in two additional Benin locations—Savalou and Parakou—and its agriculture-and-education development model has been replicated in many countries around the world. As a result, thousands of young would-be entrepreneurs are now self-sustaining. The Songhai Center and Father Nzamujo were featured on CNN's Africa Report as a special on the marvels of successful development in Africa.

Our embassy was also delighted to showcase artists. It was a great experience for me to coordinate—through our public diplomacy officer, Jennifer Shamming—a special visit by the gifted artist, Johnny P. Johnson, to conduct workshops and speak to Benin artists. That project led to a continued relationship in which Mr. Johnson formed the Benin Artist project, repeatedly sending art materials and supplies from the U.S. art community to Benin. Award-winning jazz and blues singer and composer, Gaye Adegbalola, also visited Benin, thrilling listeners with her mesmerizing singing and guitar playing.

Special Official and Non-Official Moments

Living in or visiting Benin is incomplete without a visit to the Port of No Return (often referred to as Door of No

Return), the last place where the enslaved were seen on African soil before being shipped out on the Transatlantic slave trade route. Located in the city of Ouidah, on the beach, it is a rite of passage to stop at the Tree of Forgetfulness. Here, captured and soon to be enslaved people had to circle the tree three times, a ritual that supposedly would help them forget home before being hauled into ships where they would sail on seas to an unknown fate.

Photograph of Benin's Port of No Return Monument, courtesy of Visit Benin.

Some of my most rewarding experiences in Benin involved presenting equipment and materials to communities for health care and education. Working with our Defense Attaché and Civilian Affairs offices, we were able to secure enough equipment from excess Defense Department materials to fully equip a hospital in Ouidah, an historic city outside Cotonou. Noted Beninese entertainer and humanitarian Angelique Kidjo, who's home is Ouidah, joined us for the ceremony celebrating the presentation of the equipment. She sang and interacted beautifully with everyone present, making for a very special event. The friendship between our two nations was strengthened, and development and other economic assistance continued to grow.

While I was serving as ambassador, the Benin Embassy was classified as a special embassy post, meaning that due to the small contingent of U.S. officers, we were required to submit fewer required reports. However, we were fully engaged with promoting and encouraging AGOA, Africa Growth and Opportunity Act, which allows hundreds of goods and products from African nations to be exported to the U.S. duty free. In fact, we hosted a major AGOA Forum in Benin, attended by senior U.S. trade and State Department officials.

I led our team in getting Benin to do a more effective job in taking advantage of AGOA. We launched aggressive training for local business owners and government officials on strategies to access AGOA benefits. As a strong supporter of strengthening U.S. business opportunities in Benin, I was nominated and received the prestigious Charles Cobb Award for Trade Promotion, recognizing my efforts to encourage more U.S. business and trade.

I was very pleased to return to Washington for the annual awards ceremony, receiving my recognition directly from Secretary of State Colin Powell himself. It was beginning to feel like I was meant to do this. Diplomacy and bridging waters were naturals for me. I loved what I was doing, and I felt ready for whatever deeper and more challenging waters remained ahead for me on this important journey.

The Practice of Infanticide in Northern Benin.

In several communities in Northern Benin (Baatonous, Bokos and Peulh), infanticide was being practiced regularly. Babies were considered evil and accursed if they were born with their face and legs pointed down during delivery, if the mother died during delivery, or if the baby had its first tooth in the upper jaw.

These children were to be sacrificed according to local custom. Usually, these babies were discreetly removed from their parents in the middle of the night by a designated person, usually an elderly individual called *le Repareur* (the "killer" or "repairer"). The repairer's mission is to take the cursed baby to the ritual tree and kill the child in an established ritual. Some children were simply abandoned. Those miraculously found and saved were harassed and stigmatized in their communities and threatened by peers with death once out of school.

With financial assistance from USAID as well as from the Democracy and Human Rights Fund, the Ambassador's Self-Help program supported local efforts that were trying to eliminate this dreaded practice. We underwrote information and sensitization campaigns, encouraging women to give birth at hospital and health facilities, thereby reducing the chance of such curses on innocent newborns. We also worked in the north of Benin with various nongovernmental organizations, such as the Association pour la Protection de l'Enfance Malheureuse.

Despite the campaign of information and sensibilization, several communities in rural areas of Benin continued the practice. Nevertheless, at one point during my years in Benin, I gratefully learned that a member of our embassy team wanted to adopt twin children facing death. She asked my thoughts, and I counseled her to speak immediately with her husband. He supported the idea and I then assisted her in navigating the procedures for international adoption. Those twins are now college graduates, productive and thriving U.S. citizens.

September 11, 2001

The most consequential occurrence while I was in Benin was the September 11, 2001, terrorist attacks on the U.S. I suspect that we all remember where we were and what we were doing when we heard the news. I was attending a regular lunch gathering with the Nigerian ambassador and the United Nations Development Program resident representative when I received a call from the Deputy Chief of Mission who said that due to a "development," I should return right away to the embassy. As I walked into my office, the television showed the third plane crashing into the Pentagon. The news was unfathomable: a terrorist attack on the U.S. homeland.

I immediately phoned the government of Benin to request additional security, not knowing if other attacks against U.S. interests might be forthcoming. Like every ambassador, my first order of business was protecting staff and U.S. citizens within my assigned country. I implemented the warden system of notifying U.S. citizens, and I called a country team meeting, including my deputy, agency heads and section chiefs, instructing everyone to keep low profiles, monitor developments and communicate any suspicious information.

Condolences from the government, colleagues and local citizens poured in. President Kérékou visited the embassy to express solidarity and to sign the condolence book. A ceremony of remembrance was held at the National Cathedral in Cotonou that was packed with sympathizers including the president and Mrs. Kérékou and citizens from all walks of life. For the first time, I was assigned a security detail, a practice that became the norm for the rest of my tenures and subsequent ambassadorial appointments.

About two weeks after the attack, I received a call from Assistant Secretary for Africa Walter Kansteiner, inquiring about our staff's wellbeing. I assured him that we were receiving full support from the government of Benin, that our embassy security had been augmented appropriately, and that I had taken every measure to enhance the safety and security of our personnel and facilities. Washington was consumed by the attacks; hence, U.S. embassies and consulates had been largely left to fend for themselves when it came to their safety and security. I assured the department that things were stable, and we were getting back to our duties.

Soon after the call from Kansteiner, I received a call from the Africa Bureau's principal deputy assistant secretary, Ambassador Mark Bellamy. Mark asked if I would be willing to cut short my tour as ambassador to return to Washington to assume a deputy assistant secretary position in the Bureau of African Affairs.

Mark and I had worked together in South Africa during the historic transition from apartheid, but this was the last offer I expected. I knew it meant I could not finish many of the programs to strengthen democracy, and efforts to en-hance economic empowerment. But I realized I had to accept this opportunity.

So after two years in Benin, I returned to Washington. I would be managing a complex and busy portfolio, trying to calm waters in fifteen different West African countries, not just the one to which I had been accredited.

Though my embassy staff, as well as many colleagues in and out of government, lamented my early departure, pro-fessional diplomats generally understood the significance and importance of the new assignment. Prior to my depar-ture, the Benin government conferred on me the National Honor of Benin, one of the country's highest honors for non-Beninese citizens. The presentation ceremony and various farewell gatherings, both official and non-official, were widely covered in local media.

My first and very successful ambassadorship had come to an end. I departed with more than a tinge of sadness, for I had made lifelong friends with the people of Benin and with colleague diplomats from many countries. However, I had the expectations of a new, more complex assignment as the Deputy Assistant Secretary for Africa, specifically responsible for West Africa, economic policy, and public diplomacy.

West Africa was beginning to feel like home to me, and it would certainly be a highlight of my professional experience to hold such a position under Secretary of State Gen. (Ret.) Colin Powell.

Remembering Pamela Bridgewater

Ambassador Bridgewater's heart for people was never more evident than at a reception she held in Benin for the embassy's security guards. Showing appreciation to the guards was something that hadn't been done prior to Ambassador Bridgewater's time in Benin. Afterwards, the guards felt so affirmed that they all clearly and positively raised their own performance levels.

I am blessed to know this exemplary diplomat.

—Don Curtis,
Retired Senior Foreign Service Officer

CHAPTER 12

DAS BRIDGEWATER REPORTS FOR DUTY

Throughout one of the most difficult times in West Africa, when the region was ablaze with war in Liberia and Sierra Leone, Pamela Bridgewater's voice was one of calm, and courage in a time of crisis. I learned an immense amount from her that stressed the importance of building allies across the U.S. government, interagency, as well as among African and European partners. Her lessons on successful diplomatic style and substance stayed with me throughout my Foreign Service career.

—Ambassador Makila James (Retired)

No single course or specific training prepares you to be an effective Deputy Assistant Secretary of State (DAS). Rather, my ability to assume this new position and perform successfully was the result of a combination of factors: on-the-job training, drawing on previous assignments, proven competencies through performance, and interactions with senior officials and colleagues from other agencies.

Having someone like Joann Rice as my exceptional and experienced administrative assistant and office management specialist, along with other phenomenally hard-working staff assistants, was an invaluable asset. Joann shortened my learning curve considerably, having served admirably for decades in the front office of the Africa Bureau. She knew the ropes and personalities of the seventh floor, where senior bureau officials and the Secretary of State's offices are located. Her familiarity extended throughout the building. She made certain that I understood important nuances of how things operated. With Joann and her colleagues on board, I made it through the maelstrom that a DAS faces daily, quickly grasping the vagaries of this assignment and then steering my boat on its own steam.

Each DAS is assigned a geographic portfolio as well as certain substantive focal concerns within that geographic area. My responsibilities included West Africa, with special attention to economic policy and public affairs within the fifteen countries of that region. I worked alongside fellow deputies and colleagues. Among them was Ambassador Mark Bellamy, who responsibilities included Southern Africa, personnel matters, and overall bureau coordination. I also worked closely with Ambassador Donald Yamamoto, whose portfolio was East Africa, and Senior Executive Charles Snyder, who managed security and intelligence.

My daily duties entailed administering and managing paperwork, including the writing, reviewing and clearing of endless policy papers for the Secretary of State, informally known in the office as "S." I also supervised the office directors for West Africa, with special attention to those working on public diplomacy and economic policy.

At that time, Liberia was in the midst of a bloody civil war that threatened to spill over to nearby African countries. Because of Liberia's historic alignment with the U.S., many in Congress and in other entities maintained an active interest in what was happening. Charles Taylor, Liberia's strongman president, had entrenched himself in power despite widespread brutal killings, health crises, and social discord.

I remember attending a meeting in the White House Situation Room with interagency senior national security officials to discuss options to end the war. Secretary of State Powell had invited me to attend to share current bureau thinking and actions. I anticipated heading to the meeting at an appropriate time, meeting the secretary there. However, Secretary Powell sent word that he expected me to accompany him in his official vehicle. I'll never forget being whisked directly into the Situation Room with no security check. No one stopped the car in which General Colin Powell was riding!

During our ride to the White House from Foggy Bottom, we exchanged recollections of segregation and what that had meant in our upbringing—mine in the segregation of educational facilities in the South and his in having to overcome racial barriers and prejudices in the U.S. military. Yet here we were, two unlikely African Americans—he, the Secretary of State of the United States of America and me, a deputy assistant secretary—now leading an important diplomatic dialogue and charge.

Photograph of General Colin Powell with Pamela Bridgewater at a reception held on the day of Nelson Mandela's inauguration as President of South Africa.

Civil unrest had also arisen in Liberia's neighbor, Côte

d'Ivoire. Rebel factions sought to overturn the government

of Laurent Gbagbo, which had disqualified opposition can-

didate Allasane Ouattara, denying him the citizenship

required for elected office because of his supposed Burkinabe nationality.

Ethnic tensions were rife, but diplomatic initiatives rarely bring quick solutions. I was constantly on the phone, traveling multiple times to the region. At one point, I met in London with Africa-focused members of the UK Foreign Office and counterpart African officials, reviewing strategies for ending Liberia's civil war. I flew to France for meetings at the Quai d'Orsay, the French Foreign Office, consulting with counterparts focused on French-speaking Africa. On one occasion I traveled with a UN special representative for conflict resolution to Côte d'Ivoire , seeking solutions.

During one of my trips, after meetings in Senegal and The Gambia, and while preparing for an imminent flight back to Washington, I received a call from Assistant Secretary of State Walter Kansteiner. Congress had asked the department to name a Special Coordinator for Peace in Liberia—and he wanted me to assume the role.

As the Special Coordinator for Peace in Liberia, I would need to fly immediately to Conakry, Guinea, where Liberian rebel leader Sekou Konneh made his headquarters, delivering an official message to Konneh from the Department of State. (In diplomatic language, a message like this is called a démarche.)

To get to Conakry from Banjul, I had to fly to Brussels, then wait there for a connecting flight back to Conakry, Guinea. Because direct service between African nations was limited to nonexistent, air travel between countries on the African continent was exhausting.

When I arrived in Guinea, the U.S. embassy chauffeur met me along with the Regional Security Officer (RSO), who had been assigned to assist me. Our embassy had requested and obtained a meeting with Konneh, scheduled for the next day at a local hotel.

The RSO accompanied me to the hotel where the rebel leader had agreed to meet with me. When we reached the meeting room, the RSO said, "We're here." I thought he would accompany me, perhaps for security, but he remained outside, letting me walk in alone. The room was dark and shadowy, with only a table. Konneh was sitting alone. I was face to face with the rebel leader who had been given safe space in Guinea on the order of the President of Guinea, Lassane Conte, with whom Konneh had a special relationship.

I was somewhat unnerved but remained composed. I sat at the table, introducing myself and emphasizing that conditions in Liberia were severe. Cholera was raging. People were dying en masse in the streets. Yet the rebel forces he controlled were blocking vital international aid to citizens. My assignment had been to press Konneh to call for a humanitarian cease fire to allow medical convoys to enter. I told him that U.S. Ambassador in Liberia John Blaney would similarly call on the government to cease hostilities while the convoys arrived and aid was administered.

I became more confident as I saw this young Liberian, responsible in part for so much carnage among his countrymen, listen and take note of every word. I then added some thoughts of my own. I looked the young Konneh in the eye and asked him how he thought history would judge him for his role in bloodletting? I suggested the assessment would be harsh, but I also suggested that in this instance, he still had a chance to take the higher ground and pursue a better course of action.

Without saying a word, Konneh nodded as if to say okay, leaned forward to pick up his mobile and called his "Boys," ordering them to pull back as I had suggested. I immediately called Ambassador Blaney, followed by a deep breath. The timing of the ceasefire was agreed on, and badly needed aid began to flow into Liberia.

That day's diplomatic breakthrough occurred in a dark room in the basement of a hotel in Guinea. Discussions continued with the government of Charles Taylor and with members of Liberia's civil society. Leaders of the Economic Community of West African States forged an agreement, and the government of Ghana agreed to host all-parties peace talks in Accra.

In my new role as Special Coordinator for Peace in Liberia, I was head of the U.S. delegation to the talks in Accra. Liberian president Charles Taylor had fled to Ghana to escape an International Court of Justice warrant for his arrest on war crimes charges. After Ghana resisted U.S. pressure to turn Taylor over to the court, Nigeria offered him asylum at Calabar, a city that was once a major slave-trading port. Despite these distracting side dramas, the talks proceeded. Determined participants, encouraged by the stoic presence of Liberian women, soon settled on a date for all-party elections as well as a structure for a new government. Many in Liberia celebrated when Ellen Johnson Sirleaf was subsequently elected president.

While these are defining periods of my tenure as a DAS, other elements of my work were also rewarding, such as attending annual sessions of the UN General Assembly and holding lateral meetings with African counterparts. During one of those sessions, I was unexpectedly delegated the responsibilities of the assistant secretary, who had to return home to attend to an emergency. Over the next two days, I met with the five African heads of state that he had been scheduled to see. Those bilateral talks were in addition to my previously scheduled meetings. With translators and notetakers alongside me, everything went smoothly. An unexpected bonus during those days was my moving into the assistant secretary's five-room suite at the Waldorf Astoria. Pinch hitting sometimes has its perks.

My two years as Deputy Assistant Secretary Bridgewater passed quickly. I traveled extensively, visiting all countries in my assigned region except Sierra Leone—though I tried. Among my many memorable tasks was traveling to Abuja, Nigeria, to represent the U.S. at the inauguration of President Olusegun Obasanjo. Even that trip did not come without an unexpected detour. I was on official travel in Côte d'Ivoire and was scheduled to travel from there to Abuja for the inauguration. While waiting in an airport lounge for my flight, an attendant arrived to say we were now ready to board a flight to Douala, the capital of Cameroon, rather than Abuja as scheduled. The explanation was that the president of Cameroon needed the plane. So off to Douala we headed, where I waited for another flight to get to Abuja. I arrived, safely, albeit *en retard* (late), but still able to have my meeting with President Obasanjo and partake in his inauguration.

I completed my tour as a deputy assistant secretary, knowing I had been identified as the next ambassador to Ghana, but that posting would not occur for another year. So I was assigned to Howard University as the Diplomat in Residence. My office was based at the Ralph Bunche Center for

International Affairs on Howard's main campus. My work there centered around recruiting and helping prepare students at Howard and other HBCUs in my region to take and pass the Foreign Service Examination. I loved the return to academia and sharing the story of the importance of the Foreign Service and the role these young people could play in the diplomatic life of the United States.

Remembering Pamela Bridgewater

Ambassador Bridgewater continued to be a rising star. Her glow affected all of us. She became ambassador to Benin in 2000, then ambassador to Ghana in 2005, putting her in a rare club of two-time ambassadors. Her reputation for excellent management, policy acumen, and concern for her staff were becoming increasingly well-known, not only in the African Affairs Bureau but throughout the State Department.

—Ambassador Makila James (retired)

CHAPTER 13

GHANA: A COAST OF GOLD

Ambassador Bridgewater's example inspired me to frame my work – and that of my team – in a different way, never forgetting the role and responsibility we carried as U.S. diplomats. I've kept that sense of mission, that excitement, and that true joy in my work ever since.

—Chris Hodges, Consul General, Chennai, India

President George W. Bush nominated me to be the Ambassador to the Republic of Ghana. With my clearances and vetting completed and a successful Senate confirmation hearing, I proceeded to prepare for my second swearing-in ceremony, the timing of which had been set well in advance. Secretary of State Condoleeza Rice officiated at the swearing-in and administered the oath of office. The program was late starting because Secretary Rice had to attend the funeral of Supreme Court Justice Hugo Black whose service overlapped with my swearing-in ceremony. The large group of invitees waited patiently for her arrival, chatting excitedly in anticipation of the important moment to take place.

Photograph of Secretary of State Condeleeza Rice with Ambassador Pamela Bridgewater in the Secretary's office.

My mother was again among those in attendance, proudly supporting her only child on yet another diplomatic journey. She also accompanied me to Accra, Ghana, and was present for the pomp and ceremony when I presented my credentials to President John Agyekum Kufor. It was a colorful event with uniformed and traditionally dressed horn blowers sounding my arrival and entry into the presidential palace for the presentation. Senior staff members including the Deputy Chief of Mission, USAID director, and military attaché accompanied me for the ceremony.

Photograph of Ambassador Pamela Bridgewater outside the Ghanaian presidential palace, pausing for the playing of the "Star-Spangled Banner" prior to presenting her credentials to Ghana's President John Agyekum Kufor.

For me, Ghana conjured excitement: spicy cuisine; vibrant, pulsating rhythms; Highlife music; colorful, traditional dancing; intricately patterned, handwoven Kente cloth; and many warm, welcoming, and industrious people. I knew that Ghana's pre-colonial kingdoms had been thriving and prosperous, with an educational system and written script. I also knew that with the onset of colonial rule, Ghana became a hub for the cruel and brutal Transatlantic trade in human cargo. The castles of El Mina and Cape Coast—where persons were held in horrible conditions, awaiting transport to shores and fates unknown—remain as physical testaments to this horrific practice.

Many African Americans trace their roots and ancestors to peoples of West Africa—and Ghana in particular. This has perhaps contributed to a deeper sense of connection between the people of the United States and the people of Ghana. On an official level, as well, the U.S. and Ghana have enjoyed a special relationship, maintaining strong diplomatic ties since

Ghana's independence from Great Britain in 1957. That in-dependence—the first in subSaharan Africa–was achieved under Kwame Nkrumah, who subsequently served as Gha-na's first president. Vice President Richard Nixon and is wife Pat attended the inauguration, and Presidents John F. Ken-nedy and Kwame Nkrumah met at the White House in 1961.

I looked forward with anticipation to my tour of duty as ambassador. I arrived knowing that I had a rich diplomatic foundation and partnership to build upon. My immediate predecessor, Ambassador Mary Carlin Yates, had estab-lished positive relationships that crossed the spectrum. Other distinguished diplomats preceded me, including Franklin Williams and Shirley Temple Black, but I would be the first woman of African descent to hold the position. So I consid-ered this assignment incredibly special.

My arrival as an ambassador of African descent gener-ated considerable excitement, especially among Ghana's large expatriate African American community, many of whose members were eager to engage with me. Many of the expatriates were business owners or people who chose to move to Ghana to re-establish the ties that bind people of the African Diaspora to the Motherland. Others wanted to study in Ghana, experiencing the culture and a different way of life. Some retirees chose Ghana as a place to live part-time, and some families considered Ghana a good place to give their children a sense of history and heritage. Many of these expatriates appreciated not only Ghana's convenient connections to other locations in Africa but also Ghana's willingness to offer dual citizenship (recognized in Ghana but not in the U.S.).

The never-ending demands on my time were often exhausting. My primary responsibility was diplomatic engagement with the host nation, but I also sought to establish and maintain a strong and warm relationship with many groups within Ghana. All of this was complicated by Ghana's oppressive heat and humidity, combined with the Harmattan wind and dust that would blow in from the Sahara Desert from late November to mid-March. Despite these climatic discomforts, my three-year tour was a nonstop round of diplomatic engagements and people-to-people contacts.

President and Mrs. Carter

Over the years, several U.S. presidents have visited Ghana. Presidents Bill Clinton, George W. Bush, and Jimmy Carter all made official visits, as did Barack Obama. During my tenure in Ghana, it was my pleasure to welcome both former President Carter and then-current President George W. Bush.

I met former President Carter and Mrs. Rosalynn Carter at the airport in Ghana when they visited in February 2006, marveling at the simplicity of their arrival, each descending from the plane carrying a small carryon bag, President Carter gripping as well his trusty laptop.

I had briefly met President Carter when he had visited Brussels during my tour there, which had included my organizing his official motorcade movements. At that time, we had exchanged only a quick handshake. But by the time he and Mrs. Carter arrived in Ghana, I was well aware of their active and highly productive post-presidency agenda. Their activities focused on health, credible elections, democratization, and human rights. One health issue that especially consumed the Carters was the eradication of Guinea worm disease, a parasite caused by consuming contaminated water— a disease that is curable. Guinea worm has been rampant in many parts of the world, causing agonizingly painful lesions on the skin. The Carters came to engage health and government officials, pressing them to implement small but significant changes that would end this scourge. We offered to assist with appointments, but the Carters needed little assistance due to their longtime commitments and their own personal contacts in Ghana. They were already beloved by the host nation and people.

I hosted an official lunch for the Carters with Peace Corps volunteers and USAID members working on Guinea worm and health issues. As I prepared to open the lunch with a toast to the Carters, President Carter politely said, "No Madame Ambassador, it is I who will propose the toast—to *you*, the U.S. ambassador to Ghana and to the impactful work you are doing in representing our nation." Never had I imagined a U.S. president ever giving a toast in my honor, but President Jimmy Carter was truly both a statesman and a gentleman.

President Carter's visit also afforded me another opportunity to build bridges. I invited Kofi Annan and his wife Nane to a reception at the residence of the U.S. ambassador so that members of the diplomatic corps could meet Jimmy Carter. Kofi Annan was not only Ghana's most renowned diplomat and a respected Nobel Peace Prize laureate but also

Sub-Saharan Africa's first UN Secretary-General. It was an honor for me to facilitate this memorable occasion during which two Nobel Peace Prize laureates were able to strategize together about a current conflict.

Photograph of former President Jimmy Carter greeting Ambassador Pamela Bridgewater and her mother, Mary Bridgewater, who was visiting Ghana from her home in Virginia.

My mother Mary was again visiting me in Ghana. She and the Carters bonded, and President Carter said he wanted to take a photo with "Mary." The gathering was warm and engaging.

Visit by Mrs. Laura Bush

Mrs. Laura Bush visited Ghana in 2006 with her daughter Barbara. Accompanying her were Ambassador Linda Thomas-Greenfield, who later served in a multitude of roles, including as Ambassador to Liberia, Assistant Secretary for Africa, U.S. Permanent Representative to the United Nations, and Director General of the Foreign Service. Ambassador Jendayi Frazier, then Assistant Secretary of State for Africa, was also a part of the delegation. They were transiting Ghana to attend the inauguration in Liberia of President Ellen Johnson Sirleaf.

Mrs. Bush was a guest at my official residence along with her security detail and daughter Barbara. We had a wonderful time exchanging stories of being only children, and similar accounts of our doting, overly worried, loving mothers. We both expressed angst, the angst we felt at being away from home for extended periods, albeit for service to our nation.

The highlight came when I casually mentioned that my mother would be thrilled to speak with her. While I dialed mom, I silently prayed, "Please be home!" Although in her eighties, Mom remained active and busy in the community.

Mom answered. After initial disbelief about who I was about to connect her with, she warmed instantly when she heard the words, "Hello, Mrs. Bridgewater. This is Laura Bush." Never could I have anticipated that I would create a bridge between the First Lady of the U.S. and my mom, together discussing the plight of parents who have but one child. They had a delightful conversation. Afterwards, Mrs. Bush and I acknowledged how extraordinary our moms were—and how lucky we were to have them.

Mrs. Bush also participated in the signing of an education partnership between the University of Chicago and Ghana, witnessed by Ghana's President John Kufuor and me, signed by the president of the University of Chicago and Ghana's Minister of Education.

A New Embassy *Compound*

The U.S. mission in Ghana, one of the largest in the Foreign Service, consisted of an aging embassy chancery and seven annexes scattered throughout Accra's bustling, central Osu neighborhood. The annexes provided office space for important agencies, including USAID and public affairs. But none of these facilities met the safety and security standards that had been established after the 1998 terrorist attacks on U.S. embassies in Tanzania and Kenya. And coordinating our operations for meetings and other functions was an ongoing challenge.

Fortunately, Ghana had been scheduled to break ground during my tenure for a new consolidated—and more secure—embassy.

Constructing a new facility is a major undertaking under the best of circumstances. I knew that in Ghana we would also face climatic challenges of heat, humidity, rainy and dry seasons with not much in between, not to mention the dusty gales from the Harmattan winds that blow over much of the Sahel region for a certain period each year.

The groundbreaking for our new embassy compound took place as scheduled. At last, all of our offices and agencies would be gathered together. Later, as construction neared completion—and with the approval of the construction manager—I invited Ghana's President Kufuor, former President Jerry Rawlings, and members of the diplomatic corps for separate, short VIP previews and tours.

The massive new facility, located in Cantonments, farther out in the Accra suburbs, generated much chatter and excitement among the local population. Our construction team had done a superb job, and the work was completed on time and within budget. The lowering of the flag by Marine security guards for the last time at the old chancery building was poignant, while the ribbon-cutting ceremony at our new facility, witnessed by many special guests, including Ghana's Vice President Aliu Mahama and Gen. Charles Williams (Ret.), director of Overseas Buildings Operations was exciting.

Photographs taken at the opening of the new U.S. embassy compound in Accra, Ghana, with Ambassador Pamela Bridgewater on the left, Ghana's Vice President Aliu Mahama in the center, and Gen. Charles Williams (Ret.), director of Overseas Buildings Operations, on the right.

Cultural Diplomacy

One doesn't normally think of diplomatic break-throughs in terms of music, art, letters, and science, but I considered some of the cultural programming that I did in Ghana as having an important role in bridging, mending frayed relations, and strengthening friendships between the United States and Ghana.

Ghana Welcomes a G.O.A.T. Named Serena!

I received a call one day from Constance Berry Newman, a former assistant secretary of state for Africa and the holder of numerous senior government and private sector jobs. Connie said "Pamela, I need your help in scheduling programming for Serena Williams," who was then the world's number-one tennis player. "I'd like Serena to participate in some community and socially responsible activities during her upcoming trip to Ghana." Connie went on to explain that Serena would be traveling with her mom, Oracene; her sister, Aisha; and tennis enthusiast Cora Masters Barry, an ex-wife of former Washington, D.C., Mayor Marion C. Barry.

I told Connie that I would do my absolute best to wel-come Serena and provide a meaningful experience for the popular tennis legend, later earning the designation of G.O.A.T. in women's tennis ("Greatest Of All Time").

Serena and her entourage arrived in Accra in the late evening of November 5, 2006. I met the group and accom-panied them to their lodging at The La Palm Royal Beach Hotel. I provided Serena with a schedule of activities for her four-day visit. Beginning the next day, I was scheduled to participate with the embassy's public affairs officer and a representative of the World Health Organization in a pro-gram to vaccinate babies against polio. I had asked if I could bring Serena along to help—and had received an enthusias-tic green light.

We arrived at the vaccination site in my armored SUV with the U.S. flag flying. On our way to the site, we passed through areas of open sewage. As we drove, Serena ex-pressed his disbelief that conditions like these could exist in

Accra. I explained that many places in the world suffer from such conditions, which is why I view diplomatic efforts on multiple fronts as so important.

Serena received a rousing welcome. After health officials warmly greeted her, with all of us bathed in the glare of TV lights and the whirl of still and motion-picture cameras, we began the vaccinations. Serena enjoyed herself and appeared genuinely moved and happy for the experience.

I could not let Serena depart Ghana without conducting a tennis clinic for aspiring Ghanaian tennis players. The tennis sessions, held at a local club, were a highlight for the youthful players and for those Ghanaians who had gathered excitedly to witness and get tips from "Serena the Great" herself.

The visit concluded with a lunch that I hosted for Serena and company that included local tennis players, government sports officials, my lucky mom Mary, and my dear friend Christine Johnson, who happened to be visiting at the time.

They were thrilled to attend the lunch and my mother smiled broadly when Serena referred to her as "mom."

I also took the opportunity to make a call to a colleague ambassador in Niger, Ambassador Bernadette Allen, a superb tennis player herself, who absolutely adored Serena. Bernadette was incredulous when I asked her to hold the line to speak to someone special—and Serena began the conversation. Listening in on their conversation was a joy. Ambassador Allen had the chance to speak with her tennis idol—and garner a few moments of treasured interaction with the G.O.A.T.

To top off the experience, I sheepishly asked Serena if she would agree to hit a few balls with me (not a real match, just a few volleys). I wondered for a moment if I had "lost it" completely, even thinking that I might venture onto the same court as Serena. But she said yes, and before her departure, we met on the court of Deputy Chief of Mission Sue K. Brown, who later served as ambassador to Montenegro.

I was so excited I even purchased a new tennis outfit to replace the T-shirt and shorts that I normally wore. After we had hit a few balls back and forth, I returned one with my two-handed backhand. To my surprise, Serena said I had a strong backhand—which I had considered my weakest shot.

I'll always remember hitting a few volleys with Serena as an unexpected thrill among my diplomatic encounters. We built and strengthened the bonds of friendship between Ghana and the U.S.—on and off the court.

Baseball Diplomacy

Another unexpected opportunity for building bridges and empowering youth was found in the sports diplomacy tour of former Major League Baseball star players, led by then New York Mets manager Omar Minaya. Among the Baseball luminaries and Hall of Fame players who traveled to Ghana were Dave Winfield, Dusty Baker, and Reggie Smith. The trip was coordinated by Georg Ntim, a Ghanaian-born baseball enthusiast and a senior official with Marriot International.

The rich, raw and untapped talent among Ghanaian players was honed by the clinic conducted by the visiting baseball stars. As a follow-up, the most promising players also received a trip to Little League headquarters, and under the leadership of Mr. Ntim, a first-class regulation baseball field was built on the campus of the University of Accra where Ghanaian players could continue to develop and enhance their skills.

Music Diplomacy

Music has been a great bond and cultural tool. I recognized how important it was to invite musical groups to Ghana to work with Ghanaian musicians and to perform. The Fisk Jubilee Singers of Fisk University in Nashville, Tennessee, accepted an invitation to perform in Ghana. I hadn't previously known that Dr. Paul Kwami, a Ghanaian, was then serving as director of the Jubilees. "I always wanted to bring the Jubilees to Ghana," he told me. So I made it happen. The Singers performed at Independence Hall in Accra for an enthusiastic audience. The embassy's public diplomacy section organized that visit, as well as a visit by the internationally famous Morgan State University Choir, from Baltimore where I had taught before joining the Foreign Service. Both the choirs performed with professional excellence.

Acclaimed blues singer and composer Gaye Adegbalola and pianist/accompanist Roddy Barnes blew the roof off the performance hall on another occasion with selections that entertained, educated and enthused their Ghanaian audiences. All of our visiting artists not only performed but also integrated an educational component, conducting workshops with local schools and counterparts within their musical genres.

Ghana's Golden Jubilee: Fifty Years of Friendship and Partnership

In 2007, Ghana's fiftieth anniversary of independence was a greatly anticipated and symbolic event for the African continent, as well as for the African Diaspora worldwide. The Rev. Dr. Martin Luther King, Jr., and his wife Coretta had visited Ghana during its inaugural independence celebration in 1957. Since that time, Ghana's bilateral relationship with the United States had strengthened greatly.

Over the years, Ghana has been a strong partner in democratization. With a vibrant civil society, its commitment to human rights has been enduring. Isaac Hayes and Rita Marley have built homes in Ghana. Stevie Wonder recently received Ghanaian citizenship.

Ghana has also supported a regional approach and partnership in conflict resolution, which the U.S. also promotes. It has been a valuable member of the Economic Community of West African States (ECOWAS), and a strong troop contributor to regional and international peacekeeping efforts.

I believed that Ghana's fiftieth independence commemoration warranted attendance by a U.S. presidential-level delegation. So I drafted a cable to Washington, requesting such a designation. The White House subsequently announced that Secretary of Housing and Urban Development Alphonzo Jackson would represent President Bush at the celebration. Assistant Secretary for African Affairs Jendayi Frazier, a U.S. congressional delegation headed by Rep. Carolyn Kilpatrick, the Rev. Jesse Jackson, and a huge number of other guests from the U.S. traveled for the celebration. There were Heads of state from Africa and around the world gathered to congratulate Ghanaians on fifty years of independence. Other VIPs included Gen. William "Kip" Ward, then head of the U.S. Africa Command.

Our embassy's Fourth of July celebration that year had the theme, "A Capitol Fourth," an allusion to the famous

Independence Day event held each year on the mall in Washington, D.C. Super-talented local staff from the embassy's General Services Office designed and constructed a replica of the Washington Monument from discarded crates, painting a mural of the U.S. Capitol on an improvised wall within the residence grounds. Fireworks rounded out our event, adding a touch of reality that the guests loved.

Capstone: A Visit by President George W. Bush

Nothing quite compares with a U.S. presidential visit. One must experience it firsthand. It begins, of course, with hours of preplanning under the overall direction of the ambassador and DCM. Planning includes coordinating with Secret Service agents, advance teams, communications and medical personnel, and the White House press office and media pool. Only teamwork at its best—with all hands and feet on deck—can ensure a seamless "game day." So when I received word that President George W. Bush planned to visit Ghana along with Mrs. Bush and Secretary of State

Condoleezza Rice, I knew that we would be totally consumed for a significant amount of time, planning and executing this visit.

I communicated quickly, of course, with President Kufuor and Ghana's Foreign Minister, letting them know that a visit was scheduled and receiving their full concurrence and delight. A presidential visit is not only a pinnacle occasion for a U.S. mission but also for a host country, which rightly recognizes that it has been accorded special attention.

The excitement that permeates an embassy when the President of the United States is coming to town cannot be exaggerated. Sometimes the visit is a rest overnight or "RON" as we called it. Occasionally it would be for only a few hours while the President was enroute to another country in the region. But ours was to be three full days. That's quite a long time to accommodate the most powerful leader in the Free World. However, we moved ahead with enthusiasm to make the visit unforgettable and productive for both Ghana and the United States.

During the countless planning sessions, security had primary importance. We need to coordinate with both the U.S. Secret Service and local security forces. Sometimes feathers got ruffled. When Secret Service requirements conflicted with local protocols, it became my job to iron out the situation with appropriate diplomatic interventions so that each entity felt not only satisfied with the outcome but also respected and valued.

Another big question concerned what the president would do for three days. To that end, I had several meetings with the foreign minister and with President Kufuor, seeking to sketch out a proposed agenda for the visit, including related arrangements for both the local and traveling press.

Early on, we decided that President Kufuor and his foreign minister would lead the official delegation at the airport, welcoming President Bush to Ghana. As the U.S. ambassador, I would naturally be on hand as well.

I'll never forget the smile that spread across President Kufuor's face as Air Force One landed with the words "United States of America" stretched impressively across the side of the giant 747. The touchdown and arrival of a president and first lady is such a defining moment: handshakes, embraces, smiles, cameras, flowers, flickering lights—and pre-approved, fully credentialed reporters jockeying for position. The spectacular motorcade proceeded from the airport to the hotel (La Palm Royal Beach) with flashing sirens, motorcycle outriders, "lead and chase" cars, and flags of both countries flying.

When we arrived at the hotel, the hotel manager quietly informed me that he had had new mattresses installed for the visiting party to guarantee their maximum comfort. Everything was pristine and glowing. We continued to the presidential suite, which had been checked out in advance many times by security, hotel staff, and me to ensure that every element was in place.

The president, evidently pleased, turned to me as he arrived in his quarters and said, "Thank you skinny minnie." I replied with slight hesitation, "You're most welcome, Mr. President. I hope you and Mrs. Bush sleep well." I smiled inwardly, though, as I left their quarters, quietly chuckling over the president addressing me as "skinny-minnie."

How did he know I had been walking daily and working with a private trainer for over a year to get in better shape? Had it paid off better than I imagined?

Secretary Rice lodged at my residence and joined the visiting party for the official program the next day. Her stay in the ambassador's residence became a special treat for my very competent Ghanaian household staff. Naomi Tetteh, Francesca Nuworgah, Cletus Achana, Rejoice Felli, and manager Line Micheletti worked diligently to prepare her food of choice and ensured that every element of her stay was executed with ease and comfort. Secretary Rice was an easy and pleasant guest to host. After my Senate confirmation as ambassador to Ghana, she had officiated at my swearing-in ceremony. So it was wonderful to reconnect with her. Prior to the state dinner and bilateral meetings with key officials in Ghana, I had scheduled an event I hoped the president would enjoy: a T-ball game to showcase the prowess of young Ghanaian baseball players. Two USAID officers, Nana Regina Dennis and Dora Plavetic, had served as organizers; George Ntim returned for the T-ball game along with another senior Major League Baseball official, Jimmie Lee Solomon.

The organizers had assured me that we would have the most competitive players on hand to exhibit their baseball skills for President Bush, who was not only a great lover of America's favorite pastime but also a former co-owner of the Texas Rangers Major League Baseball club. The Ghanaian players did not disappoint, and President Bush and company had a thoroughly enjoyable time. The president signed base-balls and whatever else was handy during happy exchanges with the players and spectators.

The highlight of the visit was the state dinner hosted by President and Mrs. Kufuor in honor of President and Mrs. Bush. On such occasions, decisions abound: who will be invited, who will speak, who will perform the national anthems? An invitation to a state dinner is the hottest ticket in town. Protocol was adhered to strictly, which sometimes meant moderating U.S. or Ghanaian preferences.

As a passionate lover of music, I had supported two talented youth choirs during my tenure—the Winneba Youth Choir and the Tema Youth Choir. I selected the Tema Choir to perform "The Star-Spangled Banner," having heard their rendition several times and been impressed. At the state dinner, the choir's rendition was show stopping. Everyone erupted in sustained applause; the president and his entourage were clearly moved.

Dining and dancing followed the official speeches. To my surprise, President Bush shared the dance floor with both Mrs. Kufuor and me. To my even greater surprise, the next morning, one of the network U.S. news affiliates showed clips of the president of the United States dancing with me. Never in a million years could I have imagined such a thing!

Photograph of President Bush at the state dinner in Ghana, dancing with Ambassador Pamela Bridgewater.

A diplomatic breakthrough of great significance took place at that state dinner when former Ghanaian president and opposition leader Jerry John Rawlings, accompanied by his wife Nana Konadu Rawlings, accepted my invitation to attend. I had thought that inviting former President Rawlings to the state dinner would be a welcoming gesture, despite longstanding strained relations between Ghana's current and former presidents. Thankfully, when I suggested issuing the invitation, representatives of President Kufuor had offered no objection.

The handshake that occurred that evening between the two political opponents was widely reported—and widely welcomed by both the dinner's other attendees and the Ghanaian public. One former minister of foreign affairs, Dr. Mohamed Ibn Chambas, pulled me aside and kindly said. "Only Ambassador Bridgewater could have pulled this off." I had facilitated, at least for a short time, a welcomed thaw in very frosty relations, albeit for this special occasion only. Those gathered on both sides of the Ghanaian political divide were happy and thankful to see the two leaders together exchange a handshake.

Going Places

One of the key reasons Ghana was selected for an official presidential visit was that it had been chosen to receive
a substantial grant from the Millennium Challenge Corporation, which had been created by Congress in 2004 to provide
grants to some of the world's poorest countries to promote
economic growth, poverty reduction, and a strengthening of
democratic institutions. Ghana had sought financial support
for constructing the N1 Highway in Accra, which had been
re-named the George W. Bush Highway during the president's visit. Ghana hoped the highway would enhance farmers' incomes by providing better access to private-sector ag-
ribusiness opportunities.

August 1, 2006, was not only the signing day for what
was then the largest Millennium Challenge grant awarded to
any country but also the day I first met Sen. Barack Obama.
Our meeting was at the request of the senator's chief of staff,
Mark Lippert. Lippert had called me in Ghana to ask that I

brief Senator Obama on key issues related to Africa. Lippert, who was later named ambassador to South Korea by President Obama, indicated that in preparing for his first trip to Africa, the young senator was especially interested in Ghana and Kenya. I replied, indicating that I'd be happy to brief the senator on key issues for those nations during my trip to Washington for the Millennium Challenge Corporation's grant signing on August 1.

I extended an invitation to Linda Thomas-Greenfield to the meeting with Senator Obama. She was then the Deputy Assistant Secretary for West Africa. For each of us, it would be our first time meeting Senator Obama. We traveled by taxi from the Department of State to the Hart Office Building where we met the senator, who wanted to be briefed on issues he should focus on during his upcoming visit to the region.

For Kenya, I specifically mentioned the need for greater HIV/AIDS awareness and treatment, as well as the crucial need to aggressively fight high levels of corruption. I learned that due to scheduling issues, Kenya would be the only country Senator Obama would be able to visit. I was impressed with his grasp of the nuances of our briefing and the inciteful questions he posed. I was even more impressed when I was driving home one day and heard on my car radio that Senator Obama, in a press conference following his visit with Kenyan officials, had raised the issues of HIV/AIDS awareness and corruption. I smiled broadly and thought to myself, "This man is going places," though at the time, I never imagined it would be to the White House in only a few more short years.

My departure from Ghana was bittersweet. I had traveled the length and breadth of the country, its villages and urban areas. The visits to Cape Coast and El Mina Castle on the rough waters of the Atlantic Ocean were haunting. The belief is that the sounds of the waves and wind heard in those places are the crying pleas of enslaved persons on their voyage into bondage. A tour of these castles is a must, particularly for individuals of African descent who visit the magnificent "Gold Coast" of Ghana.

My three-year assignment in Ghana went swiftly. A special farewell was organized for me by His Royal Highness Osei Tutu II, Asantehene and King of the Ashanti nation. Otumfuo, as he is referred, also hosted a lunch in my mother's honor during one of her three visits to Ghana.

My time in Ghana had afforded me many wonderful and lasting friendships, including in the church community. I worshipped regularly in Ghanaian churches throughout the country and devoted considerable energy to projects that empowered and improved the lives of vulnerable women and children. As happened in Benin, the government of Ghana conferred upon me the highest national honor for noncitizens—The Order of the Volta—in recognition of my contributions to development, democratization, economic uplift and strengthening the bilateral relationship.

Photograph of Ghanaian President John Kufuor presenting to Ambassador Pamela Bridgewater the Order of the Volta national honor.

Remembering Pamela Bridgewater

Empowerment is a key part of mentoring. As a third-tour officer, I arrived in Ghana expecting that I would have to "pay my dues" within the large and hierarchical organization of the State Department. However, when my supervisor retired, Ambassador Bridgewater asked me to step in as Public Affairs Officer, a stretch that was (and is) extremely uncommon in the Foreign Service. She emphasized her belief in my performance and her support for this challenge. It made all the difference. For the remainder of my tour, I benefited from her counsel and advice as she provided new opportunities to excel, including naming me as Acting Deputy Chief of Mission during a critical time in the U.S.-Ghana relationship. Her belief in me shaped both the way I saw the Foreign Service and the way I saw myself.

It was Ambassador Bridgewater who helped to show me that I am a diplomat, not a bureaucrat. I've taken that mentality forward in my own career and mentored my teams to identify areas, regardless of the complexity of the issue, where they can add value and find purpose. I've also supported them to take risks and think creatively, testing norms and trying out new ideas. We ensured the process never became the policy or surrendered our own agency and skills in service of a safer middle road. Instead, Ambassador Bridgewater's example inspired me to frame my work – and that of my team – in a different way, never forgetting the role and responsibility we carried as U.S. diplomats. I've kept that sense of mission, that excitement, and that true joy in my work ever since.

—*Chris Hodges, Consul General, Chennai, India*

A Return to Washington

Every effective organization should engage in self-examination from time to time to ensure functions are being performed correctly and effectively. Following my tour in Ghana, I was assigned to serve as a senior inspector and team leader in the State Department's Office of Inspector General (OIG). The OIG helps embassies, as well as departments and sections within those embassies, assess how well they are performing. As a senior inspector and former ambassador, I evaluated the performance of ambassadors, deputy chiefs of mission as well as senior heads of related agencies, such as USAID, establishing recommendations and timelines for any needed improvements.

While leading inspection teams, I traveled to Embassy Quito (Ecuador), Embassy Lima (Peru), Embassy Santo Domingo (Dominican Republic), and Embassy Rome (Italy). Domestically, I led inspections of the Bureau of Western Hemisphere Affairs and the Bureau of Public Affairs.

The assignment to inspect Embassy Rome and our U.S. consulates in the area was memorable, not because of Italy per se but because the day that I departed for Rome was also the day I got married. My husband Russell and I had reconnected at my swearing-in ceremony as ambassador to Ghana. We were married on February 1, 2010, at 515 Amelia Street, my family home and birthplace. His proposal had been a surprise, but I said "yes," knowing I was about to embark on unchartered waters.

After our wedding ceremony and an informal lunch reception, Russell drove me to Dulles Airport. Soon thereafter, I was crossing the Atlantic Ocean on my way to Rome.

Photograph of Pamela Bridgewater and the Rev. A. Russell Awkard at their wedding reception in Fredericksburg, Virginia.

The Way of a Man with a Maiden

There are three things that are too amazing for me, that I do not understand: The way of an eagle in the sky, the way of a snake on a rock, the way of a ship on the high seas and the way of a man with a maiden.

—Proverbs 30:18–19 (NIV)

CHAPTER 14

Jamaica, Farewell

Ambassador Pamela E. Bridgewater flew into Jamaica like one of those hurricanes we often learn about being born off the northern coast of Africa, expected to arrive at a particular time in Jamaica. Ambassador Bridgewater arrived at a time when the island was experiencing one of the most politically volatile periods in its history. She masterfully exuded an air of calm, cool confidence, which immediately brought everyone in her presence to an ease.

—*Rosalee Strudwick, Protocol Assistant,*
U.S. Embassy, Jamaica

I was in the second year of my assignment in the office of the Inspector General when I received a call from the Acting Inspector General, Ambassador Harry Geisel. Harry phoned to say that the position of ambassador to Jamaica was open and had been for over a year. The bilateral relationship was being tested over the government of Jamaica's refusal to extradite Christopher "Dudas" Coke, who was wanted in the U.S. for drug and related crimes. Harry remembered that I had served in Jamaica and had successfully served as ambassador at two other posts. He thought I'd be a great candidate for the difficult but open Jamaica post.

I was surprised. I had already submitted my bid list and had several scheduled interviews for onward assignments that looked favorable. An assignment that especially interested me was as chief of mission in Montenegro. I had listed it as a bid of high interest. The Principal Deputy Assistant Secretary for European Affairs had sought me out to encourage me to bid on European posts. I had begun my diplomatic posting in Europe, so ending my career back in Europe, after thirty years with the department, could function as a full circle of sorts.

Nevertheless, I thought seriously about Jamaica. Given my mother's failing health, its proximity to the U.S. was attractive. I suspected I could build on my existing personal contacts with leaders of both of Jamaica's political parties, as well as my knowledge of some leaders in Jamaica's civil society and business community, many of whom remembered me from my earlier assignment there. I had stayed in occasional communication with some of them while joining the throngs of U.S. citizens who flood to the island's beautiful shores.

Feeling aware of both the opportunities and challenges, I added Jamaica to my list of potential assignments. The Department of State chose me as its candidate, and President Obama nominated me for the Jamaica post. The U.S. Senate confirmed me in 2010. Jamaica had been without a U.S. ambassador for over fifteen months, and the Jamaican government and people were waiting anxiously for the U.S. to send an envoy. The U.S. was fortunate that our embassy had been managed effectively in the interim under the leadership of charge d'affaires Isiah Parnell.

Photograph of President Barack Obama in the White House with Ambassador Pamela Bridgewater and her husband, the Rev. A. Russell Awkard.

While Jamaica had long been a close and valued bilateral partner with the U.S., the relationship at the time of my appointment was strained—with not a lot of trust on either side.

Jamaican drug lord Christopher "Dudus" Coke was wanted in the U.S. on drug-related charges. The country had been in the throes of Coke's stranglehold in the Tivoli Gardens neighborhood of Kingston, which for years had also been a Jamaica Labor Party (JLP) stronghold. Coke was head of the notorious Shower Posse, a violent drug gang.

Although the U.S. had requested that Coke be extradited to the U.S. on drug charges, the JLP government, headed by Prime Minister Bruce Golding, had refused the request for an extended period, further straining relations. Residents of Tivoli Gardens, loyal to Coke, began arming themselves to block attempts and violence ensued.

Such was the intensity of the violence that the Jamaica Defense Force entered Tivoli and engaged in a fierce and deadly firefight in an attempt to restore order and cause Coke to surrender or capture him. Although Coke had been on the run for some time, evading law enforcement at every turn, he was finally captured, disguised as a woman, riding in a vehicle owned by a prominent religious personality, the Reverend Al Miller. Coke was subsequently extradited to the U.S., where he was tried and convicted. He is now serving a 23-year sentence at the Federal Correctional Institution at

Fort Dix, New Jersey, and is scheduled for release in early 2030.

Dudas Coke's supporters would fight to the death to protect him. Indeed, many lost their lives doing so. He was a cult figure, popular for utilizing ill-gotten gains to help poor. As a result, many struggling Jamaicans were passionately loyal to him. Coke gave money for school fees, for food, and for health services when residents needed it. His supporters fiercely resisted attempts to send him to the U.S. for trial.

The JLP had maintained ties over many years to the residents of Tivoli Gardens, and the People's National Party (PNP) had many staunchly loyal supporters in the Trench Town community of West Kingston. For decades, a bitter rivalry had made these areas "no go" for supporters of opposite gangs and political parties.

Getting the Relationship Back on Track

Jamaicans from all political persuasions were unhappy about what they perceived as U.S. interference in the Tivoli unrest and their belief that U.S. intelligence and defense personnel contributed to the conflagration that left a reported 76 civilians dead including police officers and military members, with scores more wounded.

This formed the backdrop for my return to Jamaica as U.S. ambassador. Distrust of this magnitude is not easily overcome. I knew I would need to use many tools in my diplomatic craft box to navigate and bridge the troubled waters I would encounter.

Commercial and business success have long been important tools for economic growth and development. Jamaica and the U.S. have enjoyed close economic ties due to our countries' geographic proximity and the hundreds of thousands of expatriate Jamaicans who have immigrated to the U.S. One of the first calls I received after arriving in

Jamaica was from the late Gordon "Butch" Stewart, the Jamaican philanthropist, Sandals Resort founder, and owner of Air Jamaica (which no longer operates). Butch wanted to host a welcome lunch for me with members of the business community. I accepted and was off for the lunch at the Terra Nova Hotel in Kingston.

Prior to the lunch, my economic and commercial staff had briefed me on the current state of play and some important concerns to reinforce. Among the topics we anticipated were streamlining the requirements for U.S. companies to start a business in Jamaica and assessing the products and services for which Jamaica had an advantage while helping to maximize connections with possible U.S. partners or investors.

The lunch proceeded well; the interactions and interventions were robust. At the conclusion, Mr. Stewart turned to me and said, "I think you'll be great for Jamaica and for business." That certainly was my intention. Throughout my tenure I engaged frequently with the commercial and business sectors and facilitated their connections with U.S. counterparts while also exploring new opportunities. Our embassy's commercial section opened doors for U.S. business, setting up strategic meetings with potential Jamaican business interests, facilitated through what we called our Gold Key Services.

Addressing the strains in our bilateral relationship was my primary order of business. I began by presenting my credentials informally to Minister of Foreign Affairs, Dr. Kenneth Baugh, then to the ceremonial head of state, Governor General, Sir Patrick Allen. (As a member of the British Commonwealth of Nations, Jamaica had a ceremonial head of state appointed by the British monarch.) I knew that I then needed to quickly engage the prime minister and other interlocutors on issues of critical importance to the U.S.

Our highly experienced Deputy Chief of Mission Isiah Parnell was invaluable in helping me navigate the sensitive waters that I would be treading. We strategized on ways we could bridge the turbulent waves and undercurrents that were before me. Isiah's measured assessments on the pitfalls to avoid balanced my eagerness to simply get going and to try to right the ship. I had to not only smooth and recalibrate the relationship with the government but also ensure that the people of Jamaica understood that the U.S. relationship with Jamaica was not one-dimensional, focused exclusively on countering illegal narcotics trafficking and other criminal activity.

When I paid my initial call on Prime Minister Golding, I listened to his assessment of U.S.-Jamaica relations as well as other issues he deemed important. I shared my vision and the priorities of the U.S. I underscored that the U.S. considered Jamaica a valuable and respected partner. Both our nations enjoyed the shared values of democratic governance, promoting human rights, electoral integrity, and peaceful elections for all citizens. I explained that U.S. efforts would be augmented by development assistance provided primarily by the USAID, focused on education support, climate mitigation, disaster preparation, economic uplift for vulnerable communities and conflict resolution. Other key U.S. priorities were stemming illegal guns from the U.S. from entering Jamaica and strengthening the judiciary. I assured the prime minister that I would reinforce with the Department of State and senior U.S. officials the importance of Jamaica as a regional leader in matters impacting the greater Caribbean.

I considered it essential to call on all of the key ministers of government early on to hear directly from them and to speak personally about my goals in light of U.S. priorities. Because Jamaica has been historically and passionately divided between two major political parties—the Jamaica Labor Party and the People's National Party—I also held meetings with the leader of the opposition, Portia Simpson Miller, whom I knew from my earlier posting, as well as comparable shadow cabinet leaders.

One key to my career-long personal diplomatic success has been to listen at the onset of a meeting, commenting only after interlocutors believe that they have been fully heard. This ensured a reciprocity in which officials would in turn listen to me, thus setting the stage for genuine dialogue and diplomatic progress.

A critical element on the Jamaica landscape was found in the work of the Jamaica Defense Force (JDF) and the Jamaica Constabulary Force (JCF). Historically, both were critically important partners for the U.S. in the ongoing fight against illegal drug cultivation, eradication and trafficking.

Photograph of Ambassador Pamela Bridgewater touring a U.S. Navy ship with Jamaican Minister of National Security Peter Bunting and Maj. Gen. Antony Anderson, Chief, Jamaica Defense Force.

The office of the embassy's defense attaché, led by the senior defense officer, along with the embassy's regional security office, were vigorous in providing training and education for members of both the Jamaica Defense Force and the Jamaica Constabulary Force. Upgrading their equipment and other materiel augmented our embassy's efforts to help the forces perform their duties and fulfill their mandates with optimum capacity.

Perception of Caring

During my pre-departure consultations in Washington, the Overseas Buildings Operations (OBO) officer responsible for Jamaica informed me of a potential issue relating to the embassy's consular functions. The consular section of the embassy had an uncovered outdoor waiting area where visa applicants and others with consular appointments had to assemble. This exposed visitors to weather extremes, both heat and unpredicted showers or downpours.

I immediately explained to OBO that it was vitally important to cover the area for waiting applicants, some of whom arrived very early in the morning from areas far from Embassy Kingston, which was the only U.S. visa-issuing office in Jamaica. I further explained that building a covered area would be an important sign of U.S. respect and caring about the welfare of Jamaicans visiting our embassy. OBO agreed and allocated funding for the cover.

The construction of the protective awning was a huge and welcome addition to the consular section. Widespread press coverage ensued. Commentary at the ribbon cutting acknowledged my advocacy and lauded the U.S. ambassador and mission.

Delivering a Difficult Message

Midway into my tenure, I had the responsibility of informing the prime minister that the Department of State had instructed me to revoke the visa of one of his government ministers. The State Department's Bureau of Consular Affairs, along with other related agencies, had compiled information that led them to conclude that in keeping with U.S. visa law, the minister's visa should be revoked—despite the fact that he was both a high-profile cabinet member and a popular member of the governing party.

Prior to the visa being revoked, I went to the prime minister's office to inform him of the decision. At my request, we met alone with no notetakers. After informing him of the planned visa revocation, I indicated that the high-ranking minister would be asked to come to the embassy where the necessary action would be taken and the matter would be handled privately. The prime minister said the revocation was indeed unfortunate. He said that although I had looked stressed on my arrival, I should not be troubled. He assured me that despite this action, our governments would continue to work together on matters of mutual importance. I reiterated that this would certainly be the case.

Unfortunately, word of the visa action got into the public domain rather quickly. Headlines, news reports, and television coverage about this action taken by the U.S. government continued for an extended period. The minister and his legal representatives requested—and were granted—numerous meetings with U.S. embassy officials in their relentless efforts to reverse this action. Those efforts were unsuccessful.

Political Rivalry

Jamaica's political landscape has historically been painted by bold, passionate and outspoken supporters of the two major parties: the JLP and the PNP. Partisans on both sides frequently used violent tactics and incendiary speech in support of their preferred party and candidate. The run-up to elections during campaign seasons often saw emotions at fever pitch.

I used my official residence as a safe neutral space where I could gather representatives from both sides to discuss pressing issues, both where they differed and often, to their surprise, where they agreed. Finding the middle ground to ease tensions was an ongoing part of my portfolio.

Local and national elections were always fraught with concern that the passions of supporters would spill into violent confrontations. Much of my time was devoted to engaging government operatives, the opposition party's leaders and partisans, civil society, and business professional communities to urge peaceful election campaigns, with an acceptance of certified election results deemed free and fair. We made some breakthroughs over the years of my tenure. Guests at my residential gatherings expressed their gratitude for the chance to clear the air, at least for the time they were in my residence. Even after I left Jamaica, some of these initiatives and outreach efforts were ongoing.

Cultural Diplomacy

Our public affairs and public diplomacy unit was an immeasurable asset in helping me forge a holistic relationship with the government and people of Jamaica. Many innovative programs were instituted such as the Ambassador's Academic Achievement Award (AAA), which acknowledged young Jamaican scholars and invited them to the U.S. mission to meet and converse with me. We began an enhanced focus and support for Science, Technology, Engineering, Mathematics (STEM) education by providing educational material, funding workshops and programming individual role models.

A key to the success of this effort was bringing in the first woman of color in space, National Aeronautics and Space Administration astronaut and engineer Dr. Mae Jemison. Her workshops with school students were an absolute hit. The arrival of Dr. Neil deGrasse Tyson, director of the Hayden Planetarium, astrophysicist, and high-profile media personality was also a special occasion for Jamaicans of all ages. Dr. Tyson's sessions with the Jamaican community and his visits to speak at local schools brought the brilliance of the galactic stars to the island and people of Jamaica, demonstrating to young Jamaicans what could be possible for them through STEM.

LGBTQ Equality

A challenge I faced with certain segments of Jamaican society from religious entities and other opinion makers revolved around the issue of LGBTQ rights. In Jamaica, as well as in much of the Caribbean and other regions of the world, to have a conversation about individuals who live as LGBTQ is difficult. A significant and vocal homophobic element has been prevalent in Jamaica for a long time.

Part of my portfolio was to promote and support human rights for everyone, including the LGBTQ community. Accordingly, during LGBTQ Rights focus month in the U.S., I organized a roundtable discussion at the embassy to welcome LGBTQ Jamaicans for a conversation, inviting them to share their stories with members of the U.S. mission.

Attendance by our mission staff was voluntary, but a large group of embassy personnel attended the roundtable. I encouraged our team to sit among our guests and not have U.S. embassy personnel on one side and the guests on another. The discussion was rich, empowering and liberating. Hearing the stories of how some Jamaican family members treated their LGBTQ relatives was shocking.

Parents, peers, co-workers and society in general treated them harshly and sometimes violently. A surprising outcome was the admission by a U.S. staff member who spoke candidly for the first time about an LGBTQ family member. The roundtable provided an enabling environment where details could be shared without fear.

I also wrote an editorial for the local newspapers stating that treating LGBTQ persons with respect is a human right. I argued that if a nation claims to practice human rights, then LGBTQ rights should be included. I recognized that sexual orientation and LGBTQ equality were topics about which Jamaicans had strong opinions. I also acknowledged the laws that impacted members of Jamaica's LGBTQ community.

Finding calibrated, respectful and non-threatening ways to approach the subject with government and other actors was a priority for me on this "sea" of controversial and troubling waters. After five more ambassadors signed my editorial, I rejoiced that I had successfully brought others on board the stormy waters of LGBTQ fairness and equity. The conversation had been broadened.

HIV and AIDS were among the health problems facing segments of the Jamaican population. I was charged with co-ordinating all of the mission's efforts under the President's Emergency Plan For AIDS Relief. One important pillar of the plan was to encourage the population to get tested so that treatment could begin if needed, the disease could be destig-matized, and safe places could be established for persons liv-ing with HIV/AIDS.

My husband and I led the charge by getting tested pub-licly. I later invited a group of individuals living with AIDS to my official residence for a formal dinner. While dining together, they expressed incredulity at being at the residence of the U.S. ambassador. One woman, marveling at the op-portunity of sitting next to me at dinner, exclaimed, "To think I had to get AIDS!" When I admired her earrings, she took them off and gave them to me with her gratitude for my caring gesture of dinner. I was brought to tears, realizing that bridging troubled waters takes on many forms.

Portia Simpson Miller Becomes Prime Minister

Prime Minister Bruce Golding faced a plethora of widely reported issues, including his refusal to extradite Christopher Coke. Controversially, he had stated that no gay person would be allowed to serve in the Jamaica Labor Party. Further controversy was generated when it was reported that the JLP government had paid a U.S. lobbying firm to represent the government on a treaty matter with the U.S.

Criticism from the opposition, civil society and other stakeholders, as well as within the party, ultimately contributed to Golding's resignation as prime minister and party leader. In October 2011, Andrew Holness became the JLP's party leader and Jamaica's new prime minister. Seeking his own mandate, he announced a snap election for December

2011. That election, however, brought the opposition People's National Party to power.

Photograph of Portia Simpson Miller, Jamaica's first woman prime minister, with Ambassador Pamela Bridgewater.

Portia Simpson Miller of the PNP led her party to a decisive victory and became Jamaica's first female prime minister. Interacting with the newly elected prime minister and other members of the PNP was not a challenge for me as I had routinely engaged in dialogue with the opposition. So the transition to working with the new administration was seamless.

Celebrating the 'Ties that Bind'

I knew that in August 2012, Jamaica would be marking the fiftieth anniversary of its independence from Great Britain. I knew as well that our two nations had both long acknowledged the critical importance of democratic governance and the need to work constantly to maintain it. U.S. citizens had long formed the largest group of visitors to the island each year. Jamaicans, in turn, travel to the U.S. in large numbers; many have even immigrated to the U.S. and made invaluable contributions to our nation in numerous spheres, including medicine, education, science, economics and the arts.

Despite the fact that relations were sometimes strained—and even frayed over certain issues—the vital fabric of our relationship and friendship were never irreparably torn. The mutual respect and strong cooperation and partnership on a myriad of matters of importance, such as countering illegal drug trafficking, stemming criminal activity and ending scams targeting U.S. citizens kept both our nations engaged in the common fight.

I believed that fiftieth anniversary of Jamaica's independence should be recognized by the U.S. government at the highest level and recommended attendance by a U.S. presidential-level delegation. My request was positively received. President Obama named Gen. Colin Powell (Ret.) to head the delegation along with U.S. Rep. Yvette Clark (N.Y.) and myself. Both General Powell and Congresswoman Clarke had family born in Jamaica. Their participation was received with great enthusiasm and appreciation, especially because they had each maintained strong ties and support for Jamaica over the years.

My husband and I with Gen. Colin Powell and his wife Alma on Jamaica's north coast.

I wanted to ensure that the people of Jamaica understood in other ways as well how much we valued their friendship and partnership. The embassy's public affairs chief, Yolanda Kerney, took the lead in curating special cultural, educational and artistic activities throughout Jamaica's fiftieth anniversary year. She had a unique talent for managing and maximizing the section's resources and successfully obtaining special grants and other funding to augment and support U.S. foreign policy goals.

Highly acclaimed choirs from both Morgan State University and Howard University visited Jamaica for show-stopping performances that the Jamaican public adored. They also conducted workshops with Jamaican performing arts schools and with other student groups.

Later that year, selected members of the Kennedy Center Opera Orchestra arrived in Jamaica and performed two concerts. The Governor General hosted one of the concerts at King's House, his official residence. A second concert was held at the Edna Manley School of Visual and Performing Arts. And a literal "red carpet" performance by an ensemble from the Dance Theatre of Harlem mesmerized the packed audience at Kingston's Little Theater.

Perhaps because of their own rich history of abundant theater and musical prowess, Jamaicans received these top-tier artistic groups with enthusiasm. I had made it a point to have programs that would appeal not just to the artistic elites but to Jamaican citizens across a wide age and economic spectrum. All of our cultural performers focused on supporting elements of our foreign-policy goals. And because of the breadth of our outreach, we received expressions of gratitude and appreciation from many quarters.

Jamaica had been a respected leader in the greater Caribbean for many years. So when I heard that Secretary of State Hillary Clinton was planning to schedule a meeting with her counterpart foreign ministers from the Caribbean Community (an organization commonly known as CARICOM), I strongly recommended that she meet them in Jamaica.

The productive meeting was held in Montego Bay with attendance by all of the regional ministers. It is always incredibly special when senior U.S. officials visit host nations where you are assigned. Our entire mission worked diligently with advance substantive and security teams to ensure the successful and productive visit enjoyed by Secretary Clinton and her counterparts. The government of Jamaica was also fully on board in support of Jamaica as the venue.

As was customary, Secretary Clinton met with members of the embassy community who had worked hard to ensure a good visit. To their delight, even family members received a photo opportunity with the secretary.

One of the avenues of diplomacy that I considered important was opening up embassy resources to the broader Jamaican public. I wanted school students and a full cross section of the population to utilize our unclassified facilities, thus demystify what was behind the concrete wall that many Jamaicans considered a fortress.

Photograph of Secretary of State Hillary Clinton after presenting an award to Ambassador Pamela Bridgewater.

To that end, I envisioned our embassy's information resource center becoming a place where Jamaicans without computers or mobile phones could have access to the internet for studies, work, or commercial activity.

The embassy's public affairs officer thought our center should have a name, and I agreed. During Black History Month, the embassy announced an essay contest for high school students. The resource center would be named after the historical figure featured in the winning essay.

We received many outstanding entries, but the winning essay, entitled "The Soul of a Continent," focused on Paul Robeson's 1948 visit to Jamaica, singing and speaking to a crowd of eighty thousand in Kingston, where he was embraced warmly as a man of the people.

Thus, the resource center at our U.S. embassy in Jamaica would bear the name of Paul Robeson, the internationally acclaimed African American bass-baritone singer, actor, star athlete and controversial political activist. The naming ceremony came 52 years to the day after the Department of State revoked Roberson's U.S. passport because he spoke out against U.S. Cold War policies overseas and Jim Crow racism at home. The loss of his passport, which wasn't reissued until 1958, had caused a significant financial hardship by keeping Robeson from many international singing and speaking engagements.

The naming ceremony for the embassy's information resource center was January 30, 2013, thirty-seven years after

Robeson's death and ten years after the U.S. Postal Service had issued a stamp bearing his image. At the naming ceremony, I commented to a reporter about the many ways in which culture is an important and especially effective tool of diplomacy.

Serious Issues to Tackle

Jamaica was struggling with troubling levels of crime, especially in the so-called "garrison communities." In selected parishes, violent confrontations between youth gangs were ongoing. These issues, along with social inequities, health inadequacies, and the need to improve economic outcomes for vulnerable citizens were front -burner issues for the U.S. government as a partner with Jamaica.

At the embassy, I asked our U.S. mission interagency team to identify what each agency could bring to our collective effort to mitigate, improve and hopefully eliminate these problems. We also partnered with other U.S. entities, such as the American Chamber of Commerce in Jamaica, who joined with us in efforts to improve the business climate and thus opportunities for U.S. companies.

As a hands-on ambassador, I visited conflict areas in Kingston and St. James, speaking with young people and encouraging dialogue to settle disputes. We provided mentoring and supported job training and employment opportunities, funded by USAID and the public diplomacy section.

Friends who visited as tourists also volunteered to perform social uplift projects. Members of my university graduating class visited and not only had a holiday on the beautiful waters of Jamaica but also volunteered at health centers and children's homes. Some brought books and read to children; others planted gardens to beautify the facilities. *Smile Jamaica*, the local equivalent of NBC's *Today* show, interviewed some class members who spoke about voluntourism, a concept combining a holiday with a worthwhile volunteer activity or social service.

Members of New Zion Baptist Church in Louisville, Kentucky, where my husband pastors, traveled to Kingston as both tourists and volunteers. Their volunteer work centered on refurbishments to the Jamaica Children's Home in Kingston, including fixing broken doors in the girls' wing, painting and repairing, as well as attending to the girls' personal care by helping with hair washing and other beauty rituals. The New Zion group and I also helped the students to study for upcoming exams and then enjoyed a lunch for the entire group provided by the church members.

Jamaica's civil and governmental leaders frequently expressed their concern about the proliferation of illegal guns, which were often used for criminal activity. Many of those guns emanated from the U.S. and the government of Jamaica did not believe the U.S. was doing enough to stop the flow. Dialogue on ways to stem the flow were ongoing with local and senior officials in law enforcement, who visited the island frequently, hoping to find solutions. The problem was persistent and intractable; our team continued working to seek lasting solutions.

My outreach to the Jamaican community was also manifest in other ways, including speaking to diverse audiences at award ceremonies for police, for military members, for Caribbean Aviation Center student pilots, even for prison wardens. I spread the message of academic excellence at numerous graduations, and on one occasion I spoke at the Jamaica Baptist Union presenting classic books from my grandfather's collection to those studying theology.

As my assignment drew to an end, our last U.S. Independence Day commemoration aimed to showcase all of the geographic areas of the United States through a sampling of cuisine unique to those areas. With the theme, *A Culinary Tour of the U.S.*, our embassy sponsored top chefs from Marriott International who prepared regional cuisine with the help of aspiring young Jamaican chefs. The chefs specializing in pastry, main courses and side dishes were among Marriott's best.

I drew on my previous association and long friendship with Marriott's director of diplomatic relations, George Ntim. He identified chefs who could be on temporary loan from their Marriott duties. American Airlines, which carries hundreds of thousands of tourists to Jamaica each year, happily agreed to provide transportation to bring the three chefs to Jamaica. A special grant from public affairs paid for the classes the chefs conducted with aspiring Jamaican chefs. It was a win-win recipe for utilizing our meager representational funds to maximum effect through partnerships that I had cultivated over time.

On the Fourth of July, our Jamaican invitees were eager to "travel to the U.S." via our culinary offerings. With support from the embassy team, each guest received on arrival a replica of a U.S. passport. As they traveled through the various regions and tasted different dishes, their respective passports were stamped as if they had visited those regions. It was a delightful way to conclude my tour, educating, entertaining, enlightening, and, as always bridging troubled waters to support U.S. policy objectives.

My diplomatic ship sailed out of Jamaica and into my home port for the final time at the end of 2013, bringing to a close thirty-four years of full-time work in the U.S. Foreign Service. Although the "seas" over which I traveled were sometimes turbulent, by utilizing proven diplomatic methodologies along with newer, more innovative approaches, I had often been able to sail onto calmer waters with outcomes that well-suited both the peoples of the United States and the peoples of those nations where I was honored to serve.

Photograph of Pamela Bridgewater's farewell call on Jamaica's Governor General, Sir Patrick Allen.

Remembering Pamela Bridgewater

Working for and having close access to a United States Ambassador is a dream. It's a coveted job for many, especially a Foreign Service National. During my twenty-one years at Embassy Kingston, I had the privilege of ensuring that ambassadors serving their country in my country had a smooth transition into office. Therefore, I made myself available for their every beck and call.

I was the primary liaison between the ambassador's office and the official residence and between the Jamaican government, the diplomatic community, international organizations, private and public sectors, religious communities, and the everyday Jamaican people. Another aspect of the job involved organizing all official and social events for the ambassador, ensuring all personal needs were met.

I was privileged to work with five U.S. ambassadors and nine deputy chiefs of mission. Once an ambassador departs Kingston, Jamaicans are always concerned about who the next ambassador will be. There's a frenzy of curiosity. Things got interesting, exceptionally so, once we at the embassy got word about Pamela Bridgewater's imminent arrival. Many knew her personally, or knew of her somehow. She had previously served at Embassy Kingston and thus "knew the territory."

When Ambassador Bridgewater arrived in November 2010, she brought along her charming, eloquent and devout preacher husband, the Rev. Russell Awkard. He, too, became a "hit" with Jamaican society. Earlier that year, in May, the government, after months of refusal, had relented to U.S. demands for the extradition of the notorious drug "kingpin," Christopher Michael "Dudas" Coke. It was a turbulent time for us Jamaicans. The two major political parties were in a deep divide. The island was experiencing bitter rivalries by political gangs, which precipitated an increase in shootings, fire-bombings, and government-declared states of emergency.

During her first months in office, Ambassador Bridgewater expertly navigated the political turmoil. By then, Coke's extradition had happened, and his trial in New York had begun. She ensured the integrity of the process by constantly engaging and liaising with the government of Jamaica and the U.S. State Department.

During Ambassador Bridgewater's time in Jamaica, she was always wearing a brilliant smile. She made it a point of duty to know everyone's names and important details—and she would greet everyone accordingly.

She was always hosting dinners, receptions and other social events to recognize achievements among her political allies and between countries. I always admired the way she carried out her job with pride for her country without triggering offense. I think this, and her impeccable eye for detail, contributed to her success while dealing with official matters.

Ambassador Bridgewater had her own busy calendar of events, but with Rev.'s fast-growing reputation, of delivering a sermon, it did not take long for churches and other event planners to flood the office with requests for them both to attend—or for Rev. to deliver a sermon. She was always integrally involved in the welfare of her staff, both American and Jamaican, and found ways to unite us and hear our thoughts through the many events she hosted at the office and at her residence.

To say that she served her country with grace, humility, and a tremendous sense of duty is an understatement. She undoubtedly knew what the mission was and possessed the rare combination of skills that allowed her to achieve her goals, which were simultaneously her mission's goals. Her sense of style, appropriateness and decorum spoke volumes. She was always concerned about the representational aspects and image of the United States and how it ultimately affected the lives of the ordinary Jamaican citizen.

It would take an entire book to capture and recount the stories of Ambassador Bridgewater's tenure in Jamaica. The mark she left is indelible. Today, if you ask a group of Jamaicans if they remember the name of any U.S. ambassador of the last twenty-five years, they will say, "Bridgewater." It's that simple.

—Rosalee S. Strudwick, Protocol Assistant,
1997–2018, U.S. Embassy, Kingston, Jamaica

Remembering Pamela Bridgewater

The word *mentor* is a verb, because to mentor someone is to train or guide. I met Ambassador Bridgewater before I joined the Foreign Service. She was "Diplomat in Residence" at my alma mater, Howard University, when I was a doctoral student deciding if I would leave my job as a Library of Congress music historian and join the diplomatic corps. She advised that the Foreign Service was both a career and a lifestyle and that she was certain I would make the right decision for myself. She added, "Perhaps we will work together one day."

I decided to join the Foreign Service and during my first four years as a junior officer, I would periodically receive emails from her, checking on me and asking how my tours were progressing. She was then serving as our ambassador to Ghana. I remember being surprised and delighted that a chief of mission would take the time to send notes of encouragement to a junior officer.

Ambassador Bridgewater's "Perhaps we'll work together one day" proved to be prophetic; I served as her public affairs officer when she became our ambassador to Jamaica. It was during this tour that her mentorship affected me most. I learned so many things from her that tour, but I most remember her example of statecraft and tradecraft in her cultivation of warm relations with both then-Prime Minister Bruce Golding and his government, and the members of the opposition. When the opposition leader, Portia Simpson-Miller, was elected prime minister, there was no scramble within the U.S. mission to establish relationships with her or her government – indeed Ambassador Bridgewater insisted her senior staff maintain excellent relationships with all interlocutors across the political spectrum.

Throughout my career, Ambassador Bridgewater— *mentor* now as a noun—has been a steadfast and trusted advisor. I have conferred with her as I pondered professional and personal decisions, and I value her counsel. Whether through mentoring or

serving as a mentor—verb or noun—her contributions to members of the Foreign Service have been
invaluable.

—*Dr. Yolonda Kerney, Deputy Director,*
Board of Examiners

Chapter 15

Broad Stripes and Bright Stars

When an ambassador retires, the Department of State officially acknowledges this with a "Flag Ceremony." At the time of my ceremony, the director general of the Foreign Service was my friend and colleague, Ambassador Linda Thomas-Greenfield. She presided and spoke about my career and accomplishments. The late Ambassador Princeton Lyman, who had been my ambassador during the heady days in South Africa that ushered in the end of apartheid, was in attendance as well. I was especially proud that Ambassador Lyman was able to witness my service as a three-time ambassador. His confidence in me and support of my taking on the stretch assignment in Durban paid off handsomely, both as a bridge over troubled waters and as a career builder.

Also in attendance were senior State Department officials, representatives from the Africa Bureau, friends and family who had supported me throughout my journey. I received a U.S. ambassador's flag, which now hangs proudly in my home. Russell also received a U.S. flag. I felt a plethora of emotions as I thought about so many experiences, colleagues, diplomatic crises, resolution of those crises, and accomplishments.

When I completed my tour as ambassador to Jamaica, I reflected on a career and journey that was unanticipated, unforeseen, and unique. I pondered what the thirty-four years had meant to me personally, to my family and friends, and most importantly to the larger scheme of diplomatic engagement for the United States. I reflected on the overseas and domestic assignments that I had tackled and why my presence in those jobs mattered. What had these more than three decades meant to the U.S. and to the people in the countries in which I had served? I believe I left the bilateral relationships between the U.S. and the host nations more robust, more positive, and more mutually respectful.

I thought of the institution that is the Foreign Service, oft considered elitist and exclusively male: "pale, male, and Yale," as the composition of our service is sometimes described. After thirty-four years, however, some positive strides had been taken to broaden the stripes that form the tapestry of the Foreign Service. Broader and better recruitment efforts were underway at a wider range of colleges and universities, encompassing a fuller array of students, better reflecting the strengths of our nation. The Foreign Service had expanded the number of Diplomats in Residence, and an *intentional* focus on HBCUs and other higher-learning universities that serve students of color had intensified. The U.S. Department of State, to its credit, had embarked on reorganizing and modernizing its work. Optimistically, this will ultimately mean a broader and more talented group of personnel, more equitably representing our nation.

Diversity in hiring should not be shunned and demonized; it should be embraced and celebrated. Diversity is daring to give individuals with proven abilities the opportunity to perform, even those who have not previously had the chance to showcase their talent. Diversity is doable and must be maintained to ensure that equity is not an abstract concept but is active and ongoing.

The Calls and Bright Stars

The Foreign Service is an extraordinary journey. I often say to prospective Foreign Service officers, what lies ahead is a lifestyle, not simply a job. This journey should be open to ordinary individuals who have the potential and ability, if given the opportunity, to do extraordinary work in the most challenging circumstances. It requires individuals who can bring new ideas and methodologies to the diplomatic tradecraft. People who can provide calibrated and uniquely curated explanations of U.S. policies and serve U.S. citizens living around the world. Their stars will shine luminously when their talents are developed and appreciated.

The career opportunities that enabled me to make the diplomatic gains I have shared would not have happened had Ambassador John Burroughs not called, encouraging me to "come join the Foreign Service; there's a job opening in Pretoria." Nor would I have accomplished much if Ambassador Bill Swing and Ambassador Princeton Lyman had not supported me in my assignments. They opened wide the gates of my portfolio and allowed me to run with it—and run I did.

Others were important as well. Janice Clements called: "Deputy chief of mission in Nassau is open. I told Ambassador Williams he should speak with you." Ambassador Johnny Young called: "The Durban principal officer position just came open. You would be great!" Ambassador Marc Grossman called: "We're considering you for ambassador to Benin." Walter Kansteiner and Ambassador Mark Bellamy made their desire clear: "We want you to be a deputy assistant secretary in the Africa Bureau." And Ambassador Harry Geisel thoughtfully reached out: "Ambassador to Jamaica is open—and would be a great fit for you." Being given these opportunities set my feet on a path of purposeful, perpetual motion.

Would I do it again? Would I enter the Foreign Service, embrace the unknown, encounter troubled and turbulent waters, both literally and figuratively, and tackle so many tough, potentially dangerous, seemingly intractable problems? Yes—in a heartbeat!

Secretary of State Antony Blinken noted: "The more complex our work becomes, the more vital it is that this department—and the United States government as a whole—attract a diverse range of thinkers and doers who can help us address these challenges, [people] who think critically, who ask tough questions, who bring new ideas, bring new tools, and bring new perspectives."

My star would not have been able to shine or even to be identified in the galaxy of Foreign Service officers had not many others reached out to me with displays of confidence and a belief in what I would be able to achieve.

Yolonda Kerney, who served as the dynamic public diplomacy chief in Jamaica when I was ambassador, astutely articulated the case for broad stripes and bright stars in her farewell message as president of the State Department's oldest affinity gathering, the Thursday Luncheon Group. With those "broad stripes and bright stars" in mind, even after my retirement, I continued reaching out to colleagues who I knew could do great things if given the opportunity. I knew that, encouraged by the confidence shown them by others, their stars could shine—and shine brightly. How fulfilling for me that many have continued in this tradition, by serving as mentors to others along their respective journeys.

The Foreign Service is an institution that must be protected, supported, respected, and empowered. Diplomacy is not a quick process. It offers no guaranteed outcomes. Our efforts to reduce the possibility of war and our efforts to improve the human condition may not be perfect, but they are essential. They are a belief in the possible. The ship of state will sail on as long as the brightest stars are lighting its course and the most able captains are ever ready to bridge troubled waters.

EPILOGUE

My retirement from active duty in the Foreign Service has left little time to "retire." I'm still crossing bridges. I'm still calming troubled waters

General Colin Powell and Ambassador Princeton Lyman correctly cautioned me that I would be remarkably busy in retirement with a plethora of requests to speak, serve on boards, or to bridge other newly emerging troubled waters. At my Flag Ceremony, which is the official event that signals the end of an ambassadorship with speeches and remarks from Department of State officials, I expressed that I looked forward to a new chapter of civilian service—and that I expected to be busy.

The ink was barely dry on my retirement personnel action papers before I was engaged as a consultant with the Department of State in the Bureau of African Affairs as a reemployed annuitant. In this intermittent capacity I assisted in interviewing possible candidates to be chiefs of mission (ambassadors). Additionally, Secretary of State Rex Tillotson designated me to head an Accountability Review Board inquiry into a security matter in Afghanistan.

For five years following those assignments, I was head of the U.S. interagency delegation that worked on the Obama Administration's Security Governance Initiative for Kenya, which was one of five African countries included in the program. I traveled to Kenya every six months for our joint planning sessions and dialogue with senior Kenya officials as we worked to institutionalize and coordinate Kenya's security entities for greater efficiency and operational capability. My most recent U.S. government consulting assignment was with the U.S. Agency for International Development as a senior advisor/facilitator for the EdTech Africa initiative.

It was an extremely exciting opportunity for me to work with the Navy and Army as a Department of Defense consultant on a team of contractors who were training military personnel for deployment. My role was to help military personnel understand the interface and protocols that are to be observed with U.S. ambassadors and at our American embassies. I also explained to them how important it is to maintain coordination with the chief of mission as they prepare to deploy overseas assignments. These were extraordinary opportunities that I enjoyed very much. They also allowed me to learn significantly more about military preparation for critical assignments.

While working on these activities, I was elected to serve as CEO and board chair of The Africa Society (TAS), having been recommended for that position by my friend and colleague, United Nations Ambassador Linda Thomas-Greenfield. TAS is a long-standing, nonpartisan, nongovernmental organization whose mission is to advocate and educate about Africa in the U.S. I served in this position for five years and continue to serve as a member of the board.

My board service was not limited to TAS. I was also named to the board of the World Affairs Council of Kentucky and Southern Indiana, the Duke University Divinity School Board of Visitors, the Board of Directors of the American Friends of Jamaica (New York), the board of the Songhai Center (Benin), and the board of the Sanmerna Foundation (Jamaica). These non-profit organizations focus on improving the lives of vulnerable populations. I am also a member of the Association of Black American Ambassadors and the DACOR Bacon House. In 2024, I was elected to the American Academy of Diplomacy.

Mentoring the next-generation Foreign Service Officer remains dear to me. I regularly advise and help prepare diverse students about Foreign Service Careers and introduce them to real-life examples of what success entails. I was happy about the journey of Nehemia Abel, a former refugee who was resettled with his family in Fredericksburg, Virginia and later graduated with honors from the University of Mary Washington. I advised and helped prepare him to compete for the Rangel, Pickering and Payne internships, which aim to identify candidates for Foreign Service careers. He accepted a Payne Fellowship, excited to be able to realize his dream to give back to the U.S. for the lifechanging assistance provided to his family by USAID whey they lived in a refugee camp due to conflict in their home country.

Nehemia completed graduate school with honors, began work as a USAID development officer and was in language training in preparation for his first overseas assignment in 2026. USAID was abolished by the current administration;

Nehemia's training was ended and his tour of duty as a development officer, cancelled.

I am blessed to be enjoying a busy, productive and fulfilling "retirement," and I will continue to bridge troubled waters.

Anecdotes from Colleagues

No One Too Big or Too Small

While serving in Benin, Ambassador Bridgewater mentored me from a civil service employee into a Foreign Service Officer (FSO). She encouraged me to work hard, take on real challenges, and be disciplined. Her confidence in me sparked an inspiration to always reach for the top and not stop until you reach your goal.

She gave me assignments outside of my traditional duties to give me an authentic feel of the Foreign Service. I represented her at diplomatic events and receptions and served several times as acting deputy chief of mission. I'll never forget the day that Ambassador Bridgewater walked into the office during one of my stints as acting deputy chief of mission. She looked at me and said, "This is you. You are what we need in the Foreign Service. Let's make it happen." My immediate response was, "Me?" Without hesitation, she responded, "Yes, you!" With Ambassador Bridgewater's support, I became a "management coned" Foreign Service officer.

Ambassador Bridgewater's natural and outstanding command of leadership, management, and interpersonal skills coached me on how to be an effective FSO. A colleague asked me why I put so much effort and care into developing others. I blame that quality on my mentor, Ambassador Pamela Bridgewater. She regularly recognized those under her charge, regardless of their level. No one was too big or too small.

I am thankful that I went to Benin. Through Ambassador Pamela Bridgewater and her instincts, I found my path. I recently retired as a senior Foreign Service officer. Ambassador Bridgewater was the key speaker at my reception.

My assignment in Benin with Ambassador Bridgewater was divinely ordained. I am blessed to have worked with her, blessed that I followed her advice, and blessed that she is my mentor and friend. I am blessed to know this exemplary diplomat.

—*Don Curtis,*
Retired Senior Foreign Service Officer

Paying It Forward

A mentor relationship frequently is formalized intentionally, but the best scenario is one that develops serendipitously. The latter describes the development of my relationship with Pamela Bridgewater, which began during a shared carpool to the Foreign Service Institute training in the late 1980s.

I and the woman who would become my mentor had no prior knowledge of one another, but we discovered in our first week of mid-level training that we lived in adjacent neighborhoods in Prince George's County, Maryland. In our newly formed carpool, we would collect at the halfway point to our destination another colleague in training who was commuting by train from Baltimore.

As we rode, we each shared stories from our life's journey, including from our prior overseas assignments with the U.S. Department of State. The seven-month season of commuting with Pamela, who was several years my senior with more work and life experiences, sprouted a friendship that evolved into a mentor relationship that proved beneficial to my foreign service career. After training, we departed our separate ways to onward assignments abroad, but we remained in touch, not an easy feat in an era before internet usage and social media platforms.

Several years later Pamela and I met face-to-face again. I was assigned in Montreal, Quebec, as chief of the consular section but was serving in an "acting" capacity as consul general because the position had become vacant. I was vacillating on whether to bid on the vacancy due to discouragement from parties in the human resources office who had implied that I was an unlikely candidate for selection because I was a grade below the level advertised for the position that was heavily bid by at-grade officers.

At that time, Pamela was assigned as a deputy assistant secretary in the Bureau of African Affairs. She had contacted me about visiting Quebec for a respite from Washington, D.C. She would visit Montreal for a couple of days, take a 90-minute road trip to Mont Tremblant to rest a few days, then return to Montreal a day or so before departure to Washington, D.C.

During the brief time that Pamela was with me, I informed her about the vacancy and my hesitancy, given the odds stacked against me. She encouraged me to pursue my goal and not to allow the grade concern to block me from moving forward with a bid. She emphasized that even if I were not selected, bidding on the position would signal my aspirations for greater responsibility.

I went forward with my bid for the principal officer position, securing the support of strong references from the U.S. ambassador in Ottawa and the assistant secretary for consular affairs. As it turned out, a week before the cutoff date for bidding, I was promoted to the next grade. Shortly thereafter, I was informed that I had been selected as the U.S. consul general in Montreal. I credit Pamela for encouraging me to move forward, despite the odds. A couple years later, as I pondered retirement, fully content that I had performed well during my tenure as consul general, I learned that Pamela was advocating for my consideration as an ambassador at one of the open posts in Africa. I do not know the details of her advocacy, but without it, I know my Foreign Service career would not have culminated in my serving as U.S. ambassador to the Republic of Niger.

During my tenure as ambassador, in Niamey, Niger, I was thrilled that Pamela was able to visit the post and observe my work. She witnessed the fruits of her labor and shared with me her pride in seeing my accomplishments.

Subsequently, while Pamela was serving as U.S. ambassador to Ghana, I arranged to spend the Thanksgiving holiday with her in Accra. I met her mom who was also visiting for the holiday period. Pamela had not changed. She was as engaged as ever with staff and host country contacts, reminiscent of how things were during my visit with her more than a decade earlier in South Africa.

Over the course of my career, I modeled many of Pamela's attributes, mentoring and advocating for officers who were junior to me or serving as a sounding board for others who sought my counsel. Now, even in my retirement, former colleagues and officers who have recently joined the diplomatic service of the U.S. Department of State contact me for advice about managing their respective careers.

It is a joy for me to see my former colleagues and new officers advance in a challenging career. My support to them is a product of "paying it forward" from lessons learned from the best, Pamela Bridgewater. In the words of Oscar Wilde, "Imitation is the sincerest form of flattery that mediocrity can pay to greatness."

—Ambassador Bernadette Allen (Retired)

Confidence at a Critical Juncture

Thank you, Pamela Bridgewater, for your assistance and intervention at a key moment in my career.

After we worked together in Pretoria, Judith and I, for family and schooling reasons, decided that I would take an assignment out of Africa. I left Pretoria in 1995 and returned to the Foreign Service Institute to learn Spanish, then and then went on to a four-year assignment in Costa Rica. That assignment led to an offer to go to Sydney, which I did in 2000, for another four-year tour.

In the summer of 2003, I came to visit you in Washington. You were Deputy Assistant Secretary for West Africa and welcomed me very warmly in your office. When I told you I was interested in deputy chief of mission positions, you said "We would love to get you back in the Bureau of African Affairs." You immediately took me into Walter Kansteiner's office and sang my praises to him. Walter cheerfully said, "C'mon aboard!" I was incredibly touched by your kind reception and encouragement, and I called Judith afterward and told her how pleased I was that the Bureau of African Affairs had not forgotten me.

I have no doubt that your intervention helped put my name on so many of the short lists. As it happened, Steve Browning in Malawi called first, and I accepted immediately.

Your confidence in me at a critical juncture led to a great assignment that allowed me to excel. It also put me "over the threshold" as a senior Foreign Service officer after the minimum three years of preparation.

As for our time in South Africa together, I remember working very collaboratively with you, and you were tremendously supportive of our United States Information Service programs.

> —David Gilmour,
> U.S. Ambassador to Equatorial Guinea

Grace and Wisdom Under Fire

Finding mentors at the State Department is not easy or direct. When I joined the Foreign Service in 1988, I was one of only two African American women in my entry-level "A-100" class. We covered a lot of crucial diplomatic information in our six-week training course, but little on navigating the complex career choices that can make or break your Foreign Service life as a woman and a Black person in this predominantly white male profession. Specifically, there was little to no discussion on mentors, how to find one, and why they were even necessary to advance in the Foreign Service.

So, I went out to my first directed assignment in Jamaica in 1989 and stumbled along in my career as a new Foreign Service officer, unaware of the unseen obstacles I would face in locking in my subsequent assignments, ensuring outstanding performance evaluations, and obtaining regular promotions. While hard and exceptional work is the essential requirement for any successful Foreign Service career, African American Foreign Service officers like myself learned very early that it is critical to have good mentors who will help you avoid pitfalls, traps, benign neglect, or overt discrimination.

My second Foreign Service assignment almost did not happen. In 1992, while en route to a posting in Kinshasa, Democratic Republic of Congo, I was officially "evacuated" while still in the air due to ongoing riots at the airport and general instability in the country. I returned to Washington as an "untenured junior officer," which meant I was not past the mandatory probation period and could be dismissed if not evaluated as having successfully satisfied the core precepts for a junior officer.

It was a stressful time. My career development officer, the person ostensibly tasked with guiding my career but really just an overworked employee who could not keep up with the demands of all her clients, was of little help in my securing an onward assignment. Even more distressing, I had no one to talk to about how to get another posting and thus secure my tenure as a new Foreign Service officer.

On my own, I eventually found an assignment in Kaduna, Nigeria, and it turned out to be one of the best of my career. But that experience was a huge wake-up call. I needed to find other senior officers who could help me maneuver through this byzantine career path, a path that did not have a lot of folks who looked like me, who experienced life as I had (the first generation to go to college), and who understood the importance of a strong network in the Foreign Service.

I had wanted to spend the early part of my career working in and on African issues. They were the ones that I found most challenging, impactful, and rewarding. But, in looking for mentors I naturally turned to those African American Foreign Service officers who had not only survived to become senior officers but who had also thrived as policy and personnel leaders.

Ambassador Pamela Bridgewater's name came to my attention early in my career. She had demonstrated integrity, competence, and creativity as a diplomat in tough places. I watched her from afar, seeing in her the very qualities I wanted to emulate. Her role as the first African American woman political officer posted at the U.S. Embassy in Pretoria in 1990 and her role as consul general in Durban in

1993 were well known to those Black Foreign Service officers serving in Africa.

Like many other Black Foreign Service officers, I was greatly inspired and uplifted by the work of the U.S. embassy and consulate in South Africa, which we knew that Pamela Bridgewater was contributing to, if not driving. In this sense, she was mentoring me—and others—long before we even had a conversation. She did so by showing us what was possible and what it would take to make positive change in the U.S.-Africa relationship.

I first met Ambassador Bridgewater in person while working as the sole U.S. Foreign Service officer covering Africa in the United Nations Security Council. The Africa portfolio in the Bureau of International Organization Affairs was extremely demanding, with African issues being discussed almost daily in the Security Council, peacekeeping missions being organized, humanitarian and human rights crises being addressed, and Security Council resolutions being drafted. We were also seeking to balance competing U.S. national interests as they affected our Africa policy.

Despite these difficult demands, my job gave me a front-row seat in observing how Deputy Assistant Secretary of State for West African Affairs Pamela Bridgewater negotiated to resolve some of the most vexing problems in that unstable region.

One of the most contentious issues the State Department had to address was whether—and how—to hold Charles Taylor, the former Liberian president, accountable for the war crimes he committed against the Liberian and Sierra Leonean people during his years of support for the Revolutionary United Front rebels who raped, pillaged, maimed, and murdered hundreds of thousands of civilians. The issue was complicated by concerns about the precedent of holding a sitting head of state accountable for war crimes. Many concerned observers were pressing for Taylor to be arrested and brought to the Hague for trial.

Deputy Assistant Secretary Bridgewater fully appreciated the stakes and the need to send a message to Africa and the broader international community. She engaged diligently with African, European, and American policymakers to promote U.S. values and ensure the United States stood firm in supporting efforts to hold Taylor accountable, while working to not further exacerbate the violence, killings, and impunity that had been the norm in West Africa for so long. She was masterful in her presentations at the UN General Assembly, making strong interventions in support of accountability, yet always signaling openness to working with our partners on the most effective ways to accomplish what seemed like irreconcilable goals.

Taylor was eventually arrested and put on trial in 2006. The long and difficult road toward that trial was in part a result of the forceful, but thoughtful diplomacy of Deputy Assistant Secretary Bridgewater. Throughout one of the most difficult times in West Africa, when the region was ablaze with war in Liberia and Sierra Leone, hers was a voice of calm, clarity, and courage in a time of crisis.

I learned an immense amount from her, including the importance of building interagency allies across the U.S. government as well as among African and European partners. Her lessons on successful diplomatic style and substance stayed with me throughout my Foreign Service career.

My next up-close working experience with Ambassador Bridgewater came when I served as the director for the Office of Caribbean Affairs in the Bureau of Western Hemisphere Affairs. Ambassador Bridgewater was asked to serve as the U.S. ambassador to Jamaica at a critical time in 2010, following a two-year absence of any American ambassador in the most populous and significant of any Caribbean nation.

I remember being so impressed that Ambassador Bridgewater, who had been planning to retire from the Foreign Service after a long and distinguished career, accepted this assignment because she was needed and was absolutely the right person for the job. It was a challenging time in U.S.-Jamaica relations, as we were in the midst of trying to extradite to the United States the Jamaican drug lord Christopher "Dudas" Coke who had linkages to Jamaican political leaders. It was also a time of intense diplomacy around the loss of Jamaican participation in the U.S. guest farmworker program because of concerns over Jamaican government labor rights and practices. These two issues, among others, made the job of being the U.S. Ambassador in Kingston difficult.

I found myself having to call Ambassador Bridgewater daily with Washington's requests and needs – often with short notice or late at night to ensure turnaround by the next morning. Occasionally I found Ambassador Bridgewater worn down with a cold or general fatigue, but she always, always rose to the occasion. She had the kind of personal relationships and connections with key people in the Jamaican government, civil society and diplomatic community to get the answers we needed in a timely fashion.

Her personal style of diplomacy was always my secret weapon when our office or bureau was asked to make something happen in Jamaica, like arranging for a short-notice visit by Secretary Hillary Clinton to the region to meet with Caribbean leaders about a new security initiative that required Jamaican buy-in. Many doubted the initiative would even take off, but when Ambassador Bridgewater convinced Jamaica of the U.S. commitment and ensured excellent meetings for Secretary Clinton, the deal was locked in.

One of the most important mentoring lessons I learned from Ambassador Bridgewater was the ever-present need to always value, protect, train and support your staff: Foreign Service officers, locally employed staff, as well as Embassy family members. Ambassador Bridgewater was always complimentary and supportive of her staff. Whenever a post held a successful event, she shared credit and encouraged younger officers to step up and show what they could do.

The reporting from Kingston was exceptional. I could see from embassy cables that she was allowing all the reporting officers to shine by getting out and meeting people, as good diplomats do. She also praised and empowered the consular officers, who were overworked with their heavy visa interviewing load, including them in embassy events to expand their skills and networks.

A most pleasant memory for me involves reaching Ambassador Bridgewater by phone with yet another urgent State Department request. It turned out that she was in the middle of hosting a "tea party" for embassy employees' children to teach them diplomatic protocol skills. She took the call, got me the answer I needed, and then returned to her diplomatic priority for that day, which involved embassy family members.

In 2012 when I became an ambassador to the Kingdom of Eswatini, a sovereign state in southern Africa, I often reflected on the things that I had seen which worked for Ambassador Bridgewater—and tried to follow her example. The most important lesson she imparted was that diplomacy is about the people we engage, empower, influence, persuade and support.

I never formally asked Ambassador Bridgewater to serve as a mentor for me, but she did in so many ways. I thank her for representing the best of what a Foreign Service officer, deputy assistant secretary, or ambassador should—and can—be. I am deeply grateful for her example and for her later active mentoring. Ambassador Bridgewater is the kind of diplomat I wanted to be, for throughout her long and beautiful career, she showed us some real "Black Girl Magic."

—Ambassador Makila James (Retired)

I am thankful for contributions submitted by my colleagues, listed below:

Ambassador Bernadette Allen (Retired), former ambassador to Niger

Ambassador Makila James (Retired), former ambassador to Kingdom of Eswatini (formerly Swaziland)

Don D. Curtis (Retired), former deputy executive director, Bureau of African Affairs

Rosalee S. Strudwick (Retired), former protocol assistant, Jamaica

Still on active duty are:

Baxter Hunt, Consul General, Toronto, Canada

Chris Hodges, Consul General, Chennai, India

Dave Gilmour, Ambassador to Equatorial Guinea

Dr. Yolonda V. Kerney, Deputy Director, Board of Examiners

ACKNOWLEDGMENTS

I am very grateful to several special people for their invaluable contributions and suggestions in helping me complete this memoir: Mark Olson who was my exceptional and meticulous developmental editor; Julia Royston, my efficient, steadfast publisher; and M.H. Jackson, editor.

I extend a special thank you to Kevin Pryor; Dr. Paula Royster; Xavier Richardson; Rick Pineiro; Powell Holly; my husband, Rev. A. Russell Awkard, and to my Foreign Service colleagues who thoughtfully shared reflections.

I owe an inestimable debt of gratitude to Judge Tyrone K. Yates for his daily and unfailing encouragement and reviews that enabled me to cross the finish line.

Gratefully,

Pamela

ABOUT THE AUTHOR

Pamela E. Bridgewater is an American career diplomat who served as U.S. ambassador to the Republic of Benin, the Republic of Ghana, and Jamaica.

She was born April 14, 1947, in Fredericksburg, Virginia, and graduated from the Walker-Grant High School. She received a Bachelor of Arts degree from Virginia State College and a Master of Arts degree from the University of Cincinnati, both in political science.

Following a teaching career at Voorhees College in South Carolina, Bowie State and Morgan State Universities in Maryland, she entered the U.S. Foreign Service in 1980. During the course of her distinguished thirty-four-year diplomatic career, she also served in Brussels, Belgium; South Africa; and as the deputy chief of mission in The Bahamas.

From 1990–1993, Pamela Bridgewater served as a political officer in Pretoria, South Africa. She was then assigned to Durban, South Africa, as the first African American woman Consul General (1993–1996). When she was assigned to Durban, the province of Natal (later named KwaZulu-Natal) was South Africa's most violent province. She worked closely with Nelson Mandela and played a key role in South Africa's historic transition from apartheid.

While serving as deputy assistant secretary of state for Africa, she managed the Department of State's relationship with fifteen West African countries. Her other assignments included serving as a senior inspector in the Office of Inspector General, as an analyst in the Bureau of Intelligence and Research, and as Diplomat in Residence at Howard University. She also served in the Bureau of Oceans and International Environmental and Scientific Affairs.

Ambassador Bridgewater has received numerous honors and awards including the Secretary of State's Distinguished Service and Career Achievement Awards and the Thursday Luncheon Group Pioneer Award. Her memberships include the Association of Black American Ambassadors, the American Academy Of Diplomacy, Dacor Bacon House, the American Foreign Service Association, the Thursday Luncheon Group, and Delta Sigma Theta Sorority, Inc. Ambassador Bridgewater is the recipient of four honorary doctorates.

Ambassador Bridgewater is married to the Rev. Dr. A. Russell Awkard, pastor of New Zion Baptist Church, Louisville, Kentucky.

Made in the USA
Columbia, SC
21 June 2025

59268166R00202